I0078460

Harmony of the Good News

Yehoshua Masiah[1]
His Life as told by
Matthew, Mark, Luke and John

aka: Harmony of the Gospels

by

Walter R. Dolen

President of the Becoming-One Church

---

[1] Hebrew name, a.k.a., Jesus Christ; Hebrew meaning: Anointed Savior (of) Yehowah. *Yehowah* means, "He (who) Will-Be," and is also translated as LORD or Jehovah, or Yahweh in other versions of the Holy Bible.

Harmony of the Good News:
Yehoshua, His Life as told by
Matthew, Mark, Luke and John

Copyright © 2000, 2015 by Walter R. Dolen
All rights reserved

2015 First Edition of this format

The BeComingOne Bible translation
used in this work is the work of
Walter R. Dolen

6x9 format
Trade Paperback
ISBN: 9781619180291

Latest Printing April 2023
(typos and corrections)

Front Cover Photo
John Rylands Lib Papyrus P52 [c. 100-150 ad.]
Public Domain [Wikipedia Common]

Cover Text Translation from Greek:
the Jews, **"For us** it is not permitted to kill
anyone," so that the word of Yehoshua might be fulfilled, which he sp-
oke signifying what kind of death he was going to
die. Entered therefore again into the Praeto-
rium Pilate and summoned Yehoshua
and said to him, "Thou art king of the
Jews?"

Back Cover "Water" photographed by Walter R Dolen

BeComing-One Publications
http://becomingone.org/books.htm

May Grace Abound to All

"**All silencing of discussion is an assumption of infallibility** ... But the peculiar evil of silencing the expression of opinion is, that it is robbing the human race ... If the opinion is right, they are deprived of the opportunity of exchanging error for truth; if wrong, they lose, what is almost as great a benefit, the clearer perception and livelier impression of truth, produced by its collision with error."

(John Stuart Mill, On Liberty,
Chapter 2; see the quote here:
[https://www.beone.ws/resources/OnLiberty-40.pdf])

Acknowledgment

I thank my wife Shirley Clare, my daughter Rhonda and others for their help with editing the grammar, spelling and for my wife's patience in the long hours I spent on my projects. I also thank all biblical scholars who wrote helps (concordances, interlinear Bibles, grammars, computer programs, creation v. evolution books, etc.) and critiques of doctrine, for they made my work easier. Lastly, I thank all scholars of serious works (philosophy, science, etc) for their work for no one person can think through all opinions pertaining to subjects: we need to compare our knowledge with others in order to ascertain the truth of the matter. Spiritually, I want to thank our creator for the Spirit and knowledge given to me, for without this I would not have recognized the obvious hints throughout the Bible.

Walter R. Dolen
2021

About the Author

Walter Dolen is an author/editor of several books, using the scientific method[2] including: *My God is the BeComingOne: God Papers*; *New Mind Papers*; *New Chronology Papers*; *BeComing-One Bible*; *Harmony of the Gospels*; *Harmony of the Good News*; *Male & Female*; *Prophecy Papers*; *Einstein: Light, Time and Relativity, Male & Female*; etc. These books were researched and written between 1969 and 2021. Walter has worked with his hands (carpenter/builder), with his mind (publisher/ writer/ building designer) and with his soul (President of the Becoming-One Church).

For more information about the author see his web site: www.walterdolen.com or www.walterdolen.ws

---

[2] (1) Perceive a problem; (2) examine and analyze all the available evidence; (3) examine and imagine different hypotheses in attempt to solve the problem in a logical manner; (4) form a theory that answers the problem; (5) test the theory; (6) always have an open mind for better theories or answers to the problem; (7) change the theory if new evidence is inconsistent to your prior theory.

Prologue

His Name. There is no one like **Yehoshua Masiah**[3], which is the Hebrew name for Jesus Christ. His name means in Hebrew: "Anointed Savior (of) Yehowah." *Yehowah* means, "He (who) Will-Be" or the "BeComing-One."[4] *Yehowah* is the correct spelling of the Name of God, as found in the oldest Hebrew text with vowel points. Most ancient texts only have the four letters, YHWH. *Yehoshua* means "Yehowah's Savior" or the "Becoming-One's Savior." *Masiah* is the Hebrew for *messiah* and it means "anointed." The New Testament twice uses a Greek transliteration of *Messias* (Μεσσίας) for the Messiah (John 1:41; 4:25) as well as the Greek *Khristos* (Χριστός), which in English is translated as "Christ" in many English translations. We will use the Hebrew name, **Yehoshua Masiah**, instead of Jesus Christ in this edition so as to emphasize that He was a Jew, a Hebrew by birth. Yehoshua also has an alternate spelling: **Yeshua**.

Pronouncing His Name. The pronunciation of words from any Hebrew text is not an exact science, since the oldest Hebrew text had no vowels. (See Part 1 of the *God Papers*) Also even today, when the names of people and cities are translated from one language to another, the pronunciation and spelling change.

Yehoshua was/is totally different and set apart from all. In the Old Testament of the Bible the Messiah was manifested to us in the book of Genesis, Exodus, and all the other books of Moses as well as the book of Psalms, the Prophets, and Job. In fact, all the books of the Bible have scripture that point to the Messiah. Adam and Eve were types or typical renditions of Yehoshua and the Church. (1 Cor 15:22,45,47) Paul in his letters explained Yehoshua's relationship to the Church. (Eph 1:9-10; 3:3-5; 5:30-32; etc.) But most people have blinders over their eyes and cannot see the great glory given to Yehoshua by God, the Father. In fact everything being created will have been created through Yehoshua . (Col 1:16) From the very beginning of creation to the very end Yehoshua is first. He is the first born of God. He is the first of the New Creation. (Col 1:17-19; Rev 3:14; etc.) God the Father set up Yehoshua to fulfill his whole plan. But there is so much confusion pertaining to Yehoshua Masiah.

To make it easier to learn about Yehoshua life on earth, we have put together a Harmony of the Gospels (Matthew, Mark, Luke, John). That is, we have put the scriptures pertaining to Yehoshua life on earth in chronological order. The four gospels were written by four different people, who wrote down in general chronological order their report of Yehoshua's life that they witnessed. Each of them left out some information from their rendition. Yet by comparing all four gospels, and using the general order of these works, we can see what happened. The middle section of this work includes mostly the various parables of Yehoshua. Like teachers today, Yehoshua repeated his teachings almost everywhere he went,[5]

---

[3] This is the spelling in the Tiberian Hebrew text with its vowel points. It means: Messiah. Other spelling: transliteration from Hebrew, Mashiah; Jewish English text spells it, Mashiach.

[4] See *God: God is the BeComing-One*, for details.

[5] See for example, "Similar incidents and chief repeated sayings," in *A Harmony of the Gospels*, by A.T. Robertson, Harper & Row

and he may not have repeated these sayings exactly the same each time. So we need not put much weight on the fact that each gospel writer often did not quote Yehoshua exactly the same as the others. By simply putting all the scriptures together we can get the complete message that Yehoshua intended.

There is some chronological vagueness in the scripture. But we believe that this work is very close to the correct order of events. We do believe that the last part of this work may be the actual order of events that occurred because it clearly shows that Yehoshua was buried for three days and three nights without contradictions, and all four gospels are in sequential order, except that each writer left out some aspects of the full story. When we put all of the four stories together, the story is harmonized and in agreement with Yehoshua 's predictions in the Old Testament.

Yehoshua in the Old Testament

Yehoshua was prophesied to be:
1. the seed of a woman (Gen 3:15)
2. the seed of Abraham (Gen 12:3)
3. the seed of Jacob (Num 24:17)
4. the seed of Judah (Gen 49:10)
5. the seed of David (Isa 9:7)
6. born in Bethlehem (Micah 5:2)
7. born of a virgin (Isa 7;14)
8. declared Son of God (Psa 2:7)
9. teaching in Galilee (Isa 9:1-2)
10. rejected by his own people (Isa 53:3)
11. betrayed by a friend (Psa 41:9)
12. sold for thirty pieces of silver (Zech 11:12)
13. Etc.

Read the "Seed Paper" in the *New Mind Papers* to examine more of the scriptures found in the Old Testament that pertain to Yehoshua. Examine other books that attempt to list all the prophecies and scriptures that pertain to Yehoshua.

This harmony of the gospels uses a version of the BeComingOne Bible translation, a work of Walter R. Dolen.

Walter R. Dolen
(March 2015)

Table of Contents

Documentation

nm29 = means it is paragraph 29 in the *New Mind Papers* aka the *New Mind and Christianity*

NM16 = means it is section 16 of the *New Mind Papers*

*   =   (after a word) means the word is an aorist in the Greek text, which means it has no time element in its meaning; the aorist was wrongly classified as a past tense word. "The aorist stem presents action in its simplest form... This action is simply presented as a point by this tense. This action is timeless." A. T. Robertson, *A Grammar of the Greek New Testament in the Light of Historical Research*, 1934, Broadman Press, p. 824 and see notes p. 1380.

In the Beginning

The Beginning of Yehoshua the Messiah's Story

Mark 1:1 Beginning of the good news of Yehoshua Masiah, Son of the God.

Account Carefully Investigated and Orderly Given

Luke 1:1 Forasmuch as many have undertaken to draw up a narrative concerning the matters fully believed among us,

2 as those who from the beginning were eye-witnesses of and attendants on the Word have delivered them to us,

3 it has seemed good to me also, accurately acquainted from the origin with all things, to write to you in chronological order, most excellent Theophilus,

4 that you might know the certainty of those things in which you have been instructed.

From the Beginning

John 1:1 In the beginning[6] was the Word, and the Word was toward the God,[2] and God was the Word.

2 He was in the beginning toward the God.[7]

3 All things come to be* through him, and apart from him come to be* not one [thing] which has come to be.

4 In him was life, and the life was the light of men.

5 And the light appears in the darkness, and the darkness apprehended it not.

6 There was a man sent from God, his name John.

7 He came for witness, that he might witness concerning the light, that all might believe through him.

8 He was not the light, but [he came] that he might witness concerning the light.

9 The true light was that which, coming into the world, lightens every man.

10 He [the light] was in the world, and the world through him came to be,* and the world knew him not.

11 He came to his own,[8] and his own received him not;

12 but as many as received him, to them gave he the power to be children of God, to those that believe into his name;

13 who [those who believe] have been born, not of blood, nor of flesh's will, nor of man's will, but of God.

14 And the Word became flesh, and dwelt among us and we have contemplated his glory, a glory as one-

---

[6] Which beginning?:
(1) the beginning of the Good News of Yehoshua Masiah (Mark 1:1) as witnessed by the disciples of Yehoshua (Luke 1:2; John 15:27; 1 John 1:1); or (2) the beginning of the creation (Gen 1:1) Since John spoke about the "beginning" in his Gospel and letters, it is John's meaning in (1) above that should clarify this verse. Yet the Genesis' "beginning" also applies, being true through the *Spirit* of Yehoshua, but not true through the flesh of Yehoshua, for the flesh of Yehoshua only existed after his birth. (See *God Papers* for explanation)

[7] "toward the God" cf John 13:3; "toward the Father" see Greek text: John 16:17; 16:28; 20:17; 1 John 2:1, the Father being the true God (YHWH),

whose angel (messenger) sat conversing to Moses between the cherubs, with each cherub facing *toward* the YHWH; see also John 7:33; 16:5; 16:17 in the Greek text, which may read "go to him" in English.

[8] Yehoshua was a Jew and a son of mankind who appeared to the Jews, the Hebrews, and the others of mankind in and around Israel: thus , as a son of mankind he came to his own, but they rejected him and crucified him.

of-a-kind[9] with the father, full of grace and truth;

15 John bears witness of him, and he has cried, saying, This was he of whom I said, He that comes after me is preferred before me, for he was before me;

16 for of his fulness we all have received, and grace upon grace.

17 For the law was given by Moses: grace and truth came to be* through Yehoshua Masiah.

18 No one has seen God at any time; the one-of-a-kind[10] Son, who is in the bosom of the Father, he reveals him.

Genealogy of Yehoshua

From Mary's Genealogy

Matt 1:1 Book of the generation of Yehoshua Masiah, Son of David, Son of Abraham.

2 Abraham begat Isaac; and Isaac begat Jacob, and Jacob begat Judah and his brethren;

3 and Judah begat Perez and Zerah of Tamar; and Perez begat Hezron, and Hezron begat Ram,

4 and Ram begat Amminadab, and Amminadab begat Nahshon, and Nahshon begat Salmon,

5 and Salmon begat Boaz of Rachab; and Boaz begat Obed of Ruth; and Obed begat Jesse,

6 and Jesse begat David the king. And David begat Solomon, of her [that had been the wife] of Uriah;

7 and Solomon begat Rehoboam, and Rehoboam begat Abijah, and Abijah begat Asa,

8 and Asa begat Jehoshaphat, and Jehoshaphat begat Joram, and Joram begat Uzziah,

9 and Uzziah begat Jotham, and Jotham begat Ahaz, and Ahaz begat Hezekiah,

10 and Hezekiah begat Manasseh, and Manasseh begat Amon, and Amon begat Josiah,

11 and Josiah begat Jeconiah and his brethren, at the time of the carrying away of Babylon.

12 And after the carrying away of Babylon, Jeconiah begat Shealtiel, and Shealtiel begat Zerubbabel,

13 and Zerubbabel begat Abiud, and Abiud begat Eliakim, and Eliakim begat Azor,

14 and Azor begat Zadok, and Zadok begat Akim, and Akim begat Eliud,

15 and Eliud begat Eleazar, and Eleazar begat Matthan, and Matthan begat Jacob,

16 and Jacob begat Joseph, [the father[11] of Mary,] of whom [Mary] was born Yehoshua, who is called Masiah.

17 All the generations, therefore, from Abraham to David [were] **fourteen generations**; and from David until the carrying away of Babylon, **fourteen generations**; and from the carrying away of Babylon unto the Masiah, **fourteen generations**.

Genealogy of Yehoshua

From Joseph, His supposed Father

Luke 3:23 And Yehoshua himself was beginning to be about of years thirty; being as was supposed son of Joseph; of Eli,

24 of Matthat, of Levi, of Melki, of Jannai, of Joseph,

25 of Mattathias, of Amos, of Nahum, of Esli, of Naggai,

---

[9] GK: *monogenes*

[10] GK: *monogenes*

[11] Two Josephs: one her father; a different one her husband. See Hebrew text as found by Nehemia Gordon

26 of Maath, of Mattathias, of Semei, of Joseph, of Judah,

27 of Joanna, of Rhesa, of Zerubbabel, of Shealtiel, of Neri,

28 of Melchi, of Addi, of Cosam, of Elmodam, of Er,

29 of Jose, of Eliezer, of Jorim, of Matthat, of Levi,

30 of Simeon, of Judah, of Joseph, of Jonan, of Eliakim,

31 of Melea, of Menan, of Mattatha, of Nathan, of David,

32 of Jesse, of Obed, of Boaz, of Salmon, of Nahshon,

33 of Amminadab, of Ram, of Hezron, of Perez, of Judah,

34 of Jacob, of Isaac, of Abraham, of Terah, of Nahor,

35 of Serug, of Reu, of Peleg, of Eber, of Salah,

36 of Cainan, of Arphaxad, of Shem, of Noah, of Lamech,

37 of Methuselah, of Enoch, of Jared, of Mahalaleel, of Cainan,

38 of Enos, of Seth, of Adam, of the God.

John the Baptist's Birth Foretold

Luke 1:5 There was in the days of Herod, the king of Judea, a certain priest, by name Zacharias, of the course of Abijah, and his wife of the daughters of Aaron, and her name Elizabeth.

6 And they were both just before the God, walking in all the commandments and ordinances of the Lord blameless.

7 And they had no child, because Elizabeth was barren, and they were both advanced in years.

8 And it came to pass, as he fulfilled his priestly service before the God in the order of his course,

9 it fell to him by lot, according to the custom of the priesthood, to enter into the temple of the Lord to burn incense.

10 And all the multitude of the people were praying outside at the hour of incense.

11 And an angel of the Lord appeared to him, standing on the right of the altar of incense.

12 And Zacharias was troubled, seeing him and fear fell upon him.

13 But the angel said to him, Fear not, Zacharias, because your supplication has been heard, and your wife Elizabeth shall bear you a son, and you shall call his name John.

14 And he shall be to you joy and rejoicing, and many shall rejoice at his birth.

15 For he shall be great before the Lord, and he shall drink no wine nor strong drink; and he shall be filled with the Holy Spirit, even from his mother's womb.

16 And many of the sons of Israel shall he turn to the Lord their God.

17 And he shall go before him in the spirit and power of Elijah, to turn hearts of fathers to children, and disobedient ones to the thoughts of just [men] to make ready for the Lord a prepared people.

Zechariah Made Speechless

Luke 1:18 And Zacharias said to the angel, How shall I know this, for I am an old man, and my wife advanced in years?

19 And the angel answering, said to him, I am Gabriel, who has been standing before the God, and I have been sent to speak to you, and to bring the good news to you;

20 and behold, you shall be silent and not able to speak, till the day in which these things shall take place, because you have not believed my words, which shall be fulfilled in their time.

21 And the people were awaiting Zacharias, and they wondered at his delaying in the temple.

22 But when he came out he could not speak to them, and they recognized that he had seen a vision in the temple. And he was making signs to them, and continued mute.

23 And it came to pass, when the days of his service were completed, he departed to his house.

24 Now after these days, Elizabeth his wife conceived, and hid herself five months, saying,

25 Thus has the Lord done to me in [these] days in which he looked upon [me] to take away my reproach among men.

Mary's Conception

26 But in the sixth month, the angel Gabriel was sent by the God to a city of Galilee, of which the name [was] Nazareth,

27 to a virgin betrothed to a man whose name [was] Joseph, of the house of David; and the virgin's name [was] Mary.

28 And the angel came in to her, and said, Hail, [you] favored one! the Lord [is] with you: [blessed are you among women]

29 But she, [seeing] [the angel] was troubled at his word, and reasoned in her mind what this salutation might be.

30 And the angel said to her, Fear not, Mary, for you have found favor with the God;

31 and behold, you shall conceive in the womb and bear a son, and you shall call his name Yehoshua.

32 He shall be great, and shall be called Son of the Highest; and the Lord the God shall give him the throne of David his father;

33 and he shall reign over the house of Jacob into the ages [aeons] and of his kingdom there shall not be an end.

34 But Mary said to the angel, How shall this be, since I know not a man?

35 And the angel answering said to her, the Holy Spirit shall come upon you, and power of the Highest overshadow you, wherefore the holy thing also which shall be born shall be called Son of God.

36 And behold, Elizabeth, your kinswoman, she also has conceived a son in her old age, and this is the sixth month to her that was called barren:

37 for no word shall be impossible with the God.

38 And Mary said, Behold the maid of the Lord; be it to me according to your word. And the angel departed from her.

Mary goes to see Elizabeth

39 And Mary, rising up in those days, went into the hill country with haste, to a city of Judah,

40 and entered into the house of Zacharias, and saluted Elizabeth.

41 And it came to pass, as Elizabeth heard the salutation of Mary, the babe leaped in her womb; and Elizabeth was filled with the Holy Spirit,

42 and cried out with a loud voice and said, Blessed [are] you among women, and blessed the fruit of your womb.

43 And why [is] this to me, that the mother of my Lord should come to me?

44 For behold, as the voice of your salutation sounded in my ears, the babe leaped with joy in my womb.

45 And blessed [is] she that has believed, for there shall be a fulfilment of the things spoken to her from the Lord.

Mary Praises God

46 And Mary said, My soul magnifies the Lord,

47 and my spirit has rejoiced in the God my Savior.

48 For he has looked upon the low estate of his maid; for behold, from henceforth all generations shall call me blessed.

49 For the Mighty One has done to me great things, and holy [is] his name;

50 and his mercy [is] to generations and generations to them that fear him.

51 He has worked strength with his arm; he has scattered haughty [ones] in the thought of their heart.

52 He has put down rulers from thrones, and exalted the lowly.

53 He has filled the hungry with good things, and sent away the rich empty.

54 He has helped Israel his servant, in order to remember mercy,

55 as he spoke to our fathers, to Abraham and to his seed into the aeon.

56 And Mary abode with her about three months, and returned to her house.

John the Baptist is Born

57 But the time was fulfilled for Elizabeth that she should bring forth, and she gave birth to a son.

58 And her neighbors and kinsfolk heard that the Lord had magnified his mercy with her, and they rejoiced with her.

59 And it came to pass on the eighth day they came to circumcise the child, and they called it after the name of his father, Zacharias.

60 And his mother answering said, No; but he shall be called John.

61 And they said to her, There is no one among your kinsfolk who is called by this name.

62 And they made signs to his father as to what he might wish it to be called.

63 And having asked for a writing-table, he wrote saying, John is his name. And they all wondered.

64 And his mouth was opened immediately, and his tongue, and he spoke, blessing the God.

65 And fear came upon all who dwelt round about them; and in the whole hill-country of Judea all these things were the subject of conversation.

66 And all who heard them laid them up in their heart, saying, What then will this child be? And the Lord's hand was with him.

Zechariah Prophesies

67 And Zacharias his father was filled with the Holy Spirit, and prophesied, saying,

68 Blessed be the Lord God of Israel, because he has visited and worked redemption for his people,

69 and raised up a horn of deliverance for us in the house of David his servant;

70 as he spoke by the mouth of his holy prophets, who have been since the world began;

71 deliverance from our enemies and out of the hand of all who hate us;

72 to fulfil mercy with our fathers and remember his holy covenant

73 the oath which he swore to Abraham our father,

74 to give us, that, saved out of the hand of our enemies, we should serve him without fear

75 in piety and righteousness before him all our days.

76 And you, child, shall be called the prophet of the Highest; for you shall go before the face of the Lord to make ready his ways;

77 to give knowledge of deliverance to his people by the forgiveness of their sins

78 on account of the tender mercy of our God; wherein the dayspring from on high has visited us,

79 to shine upon them who were sitting in darkness and in the shadow of death, to guide our feet into the way of peace.

80 --And the child grew and was strengthened in spirit; and he was in the deserts until the day of his showing to Israel.

Joseph Told of Conception

Matt 1:18 Now the birth of Yehoshua Masiah was thus: His mother, Mary, that is, having been betrothed to Joseph, before they came together, she was found to be with child of the Holy Spirit.

19 But Joseph, her husband, being a righteous [man] and unwilling to expose her publicly, purposed to have put her away secretly;

20 but while he pondered on these things, behold, an angel of the Lord appeared to him in a dream, saying, Joseph, son of David, fear not to take to [you] Mary, your wife, for that which is begotten in her is of the Holy Spirit.

21 And she shall bring forth a son, and you shall call his name Yehoshua, for he shall save his people from their sins.

22 Now all this came to pass that that might be fulfilled which was spoken by the Lord, through the prophet, saying,

23 Behold, the virgin shall be with child, and shall bring forth a son, and they shall call his name Emmanuel, which is, being interpreted, 'the God with us.'

24 But Joseph, having awoke up from his sleep, did as the angel of the Lord had enjoined him, and took to him his wife,

25 and knew her not until she had brought forth her firstborn son: and he called his name Yehoshua.

Yehoshua the Messiah is Born

Luke 2:1 But it came to pass in those days that a decree went out from Caesar Augustus, that a census should be made of all the habitable world.

2 The census itself first took place when Cyrenius had the government of Syria.

3 And all went to be inscribed in the census roll, each to his own city:

4 and Joseph also went up from Galilee out of the city Nazareth to Judea, to David's city, the which is called Bethlehem, because he was of the house and family of David,

5 to be inscribed in the census roll with Mary who was betrothed to him [as his] wife, she being great with child.

6 And it came to pass, while they were there, the days of her giving birth [to her child] were fulfilled,

7 and she brought forth her first-born son, and wrapped him up in swaddling-clothes and laid him in the manger, because there was no room for them in the inn.

Angel of the Lord Announces the Good News of Yehoshua's Birth

8 And there were shepherds in that country abiding outside, and keeping watch by night over their flock.

9 And lo, an angel of the Lord was there by them, and the glory of the Lord shone around them, and they feared [with] great fear.

10 And the angel said to them, Fear not, for behold, I announce to you good news of great joy, which shall be to all the people;

11 for today a Savior has been born to you in David's city, who is Masiah the Lord.

12 And this is the sign to you: you shall find a babe wrapped in swaddling-clothes, and lying in a manger.

Angels Praise

13 And suddenly there was with the angel a multitude of the heavenly host, praising the God and saying,

14 Glory to God in the highest, and on earth peace among men of good will.

Shepherds Visit Yehoshua

15 And it came to pass, as the angels departed from them into heaven, that the shepherds said to one another, Let us make our way then now as far as Bethlehem, and let us see this thing that is come to pass, which the Lord has made known to us.

16 And they came with haste, and found both Mary and Joseph, and the babe lying in the manger;

17 and having seen [it] they made known about the country the thing which had been said to them concerning this child.

18 And all who heard [it] wondered at the things said to them by the shepherds.

19 But Mary kept all these things [in her mind] pondering [them] in her heart.

20 And the shepherds returned, glorifying and praising the God for all things which they had heard and seen, as it had been said to them.

Yehoshua Circumcised and Named

21 And when eight days were fulfilled for circumcising him, his name was called Yehoshua, which was the name given by the angel before he had been conceived in the womb.

Yehoshua in the Temple

22 And when the days were fulfilled for their purifying according to the law of Moses, they brought him to Jerusalem to present him to the Lord

23 as it is written in the law of the Lord: Every male that opens the womb shall be called holy to the Lord,

24 and to offer a sacrifice according to what is said in the law of the Lord: A pair of turtle doves, or two young pigeons.

Simeon's Joy

25 And behold, there was a man in Jerusalem whose name was Simeon; and this man was just and pious, awaiting the consolation of Israel, and the Holy Spirit was upon him.

26 And it was divinely communicated to him by the Holy Spirit, that he should not see death before he should see the Lord's Masiah.

27 And he came in the Spirit into the temple; and as the parents brought in the child Yehoshua that they might do for him according to the custom of the law,

28 he received him into his arms, and blessed the God, and said,

29 Lord, now you let your servant go, according to your word, in peace;

30 for mine eyes have seen your salvation,

31 which you have prepared before the face of all peoples;

32 a light for revelation of the Gentiles and the glory of your people Israel.

33 And his father and mother wondered at the things which were said concerning him.

34 And Simeon blessed them, and said to Mary his mother, Lo, this [child] is set for the fall and rising up of many in Israel, and for a sign spoken against;

35 and even a sword shall go through your own soul; so that the thoughts may be revealed from many hearts.

Anna a Prophetess

36 And there was a prophetess, Anna, daughter of Phanuel, of the tribe of Asher, who was far advanced in years, having lived with [her] husband seven years from her virginity,

37 and herself a widow up to eighty-four years; who did not depart from the temple, serving night and day with fasting and prayers;

38 and she coming up the same hour gave praise to the Lord, and spoke of him to all those who waited for redemption in Jerusalem.

Wise men and Yehoshua

Matt 2:1 Now Yehoshua having been born in Bethlehem of Judea, in the days of Herod the king, behold magi from the east arrived at Jerusalem, saying,

2 Where is the king of the Jews that has been born? for we have seen his star in the east, and have come to do him homage.

3 But Herod the king having heard [of it] was troubled, and all Jerusalem with him;

4 and, assembling all the chief priests and scribes of the people, he inquired of them where the Masiah should be born.

5 And they said to him, In Bethlehem of Judea; for thus it is written through the prophet:

> 6 And you Bethlehem, land of Judah, are in no way the least among the governors of Judah; for out of you shall go forth a leader who shall shepherd my people Israel.

7 Then Herod, having secretly called the magi, inquired of them accurately the time of the star that was appearing;

8 and having sent them to Bethlehem, said, Go, search out accurately concerning the child, and when you shall have found him bring me back word, so that I also may come and do him homage.

9 And they having heard the king went their way; and lo, the star, which they had seen in the east, went before them until it came and stood over the place where the little child was.

10 And when they saw the star they rejoiced with exceeding great joy.

11 And having come into the house they saw the little child with Mary his mother, and falling down did him homage. And having opened their treasures, they offered to him gifts, gold, and frankincense, and myrrh.

12 And being divinely instructed in a dream not to return to Herod, they departed into their own country another way.

Yehoshua Taken to Egypt to Flee Herod

13 Now, they having departed, behold, an angel of the Lord appears in a dream to Joseph, saying, Arise, take to [you] the little child and his mother, and flee into Egypt, and be there until I shall tell you; for Herod will seek the little child to destroy it.

14 And, having arisen, he took to him the little child and his mother by night, and departed into Egypt.

15 And he was there until the death of Herod, that that might be fulfilled which was spoken by the Lord through the prophet, saying, Out of Egypt have I called my son.

Herod kills Children

16 Then Herod, seeing that he had been mocked by the magi, was greatly enraged; and sent and slew all the boys which [were] in Bethlehem, and in all its borders, from two years and under, according to the time which he had carefully ascertained from the magi.

17 Then was fulfilled that which was spoken through Jeremiah the prophet, saying,

> 18 A voice has been heard in Rama, weeping, and great lamentation: Rachel weeping [for] her children, and would not be comforted, because they are not.

Herod Dies, Yehoshua returns to Nazareth

19 But Herod having died, behold, an angel of the Lord appears in a dream to Joseph in Egypt, saying,

20 Arise, take to [you] the little child and its mother, and go into the land of Israel: for they who sought the soul of the little child are dead.

21 And he arose and took to him the little child and its mother, and came into the land of Israel;

22 but having heard that 'Archelaus reigns over Judea, instead of Herod his father', he was afraid to go there; and having been divinely instructed in a dream, he went away into the parts of Galilee,

23 and came and dwelt in a town called Nazareth; so that that should be fulfilled which was spoken through the prophets, He shall be called a Nazaraene.

Luke 2:39 And when they had completed all things according to the law of the Lord, they returned to Galilee to their own city Nazareth.

40 And the child grew and became strong [in spirit] filled with wisdom, and God's grace was upon him.

52 And Yehoshua advanced in wisdom and stature, and in grace with God and men.

Yehoshua at 12 Years

Yehoshua at Twelve Years Visits Jerusalem at the Passover

41 And his parents went yearly to Jerusalem at the feast of the Passover.

42 And when he was of years twelve, and they went up [to Jerusalem] according to the custom of the feast

43 and had completed the days, as they returned, the boy Yehoshua remained behind in Jerusalem, and his parents knew not [of it]

44 but, supposing him to be in the company that journeyed together, they went a day's journey, and sought him among their relations and acquaintances:

45 and not having found him they returned to Jerusalem seeking him.

46 And it came to pass, after three days they found him in the temple, sitting in the midst of the teachers and hearing them and asking them questions.

47 And all who heard him were astonished at his understanding and answers.

48 And when they saw him they were amazed: and his mother said to him, Child, why have you dealt thus with us? behold, your father and I have sought you distressed.

49 And he said to them, Why [is it] that you have sought me? did you not know that I ought to be [occupied] in my Father's business?

50 And they understood not the thing that he said to them.

Yehoshua Grew up in Nazareth

51 And he went down with them and came to Nazareth, and he was in subjection to them. And his mother kept all these things in her heart.

John the Baptist's Mission

John's Mission

Luke 3:1 Now in the fifteenth year of the government of Tiberius Caesar, Pontius Pilate being governor of Judea, and Herod tetrarch of Galilee, and Philip his brother tetrarch of Ituraea and the region of Trachonitis, and Lysanias tetrarch of Abilene,

2 in the high priesthood of Annas and Caiaphas, the word of God came upon John, the son of Zacharias, in the wilderness.

3 And he came into all the district round the Jordan, preaching the baptism of repentance for the forgiveness of sins,

4 as it is written in the book of the words of Isaiah the prophet: Voice of one crying in the wilderness: Prepare you the way of the Lord, make straight his paths.

5 Every gorge shall be filled up, and every mountain and hill shall be brought low, and the crooked [places] shall become a straight [path] and the rough places smooth ways,

6 and all flesh shall see the salvation of the God.

John Baptizes People with the Water of the Jordan River

Matt 3:4 And John himself had his garment of camel's hair, and a leathern girdle about his loins, and his nourishment was locusts and wild honey.

5 Then went out to him Jerusalem, and all Judea, and all the country round the Jordan,

6 and were baptized by him in the Jordan, acknowledging their sins.

John Teaches Repentance

Luke 3:7 He said therefore to the crowds which went out to be baptized by him, Offspring of vipers, who has forewarned you to flee from the coming wrath?

8 Produce therefore fruits worthy of repentance and begin not to say in yourselves, We have Abraham for [our] father, for I say unto you that the God is able of these stones to raise up children to Abraham.

9 And already also the axe is applied to the root of the trees; every tree therefore not producing good fruit is cut down and cast into the fire.

10 And the crowds asked him saying, What should we do then?

11 And he answering says to them, He that has two body-coats, let him give to him that has none; and he that has food, let him do likewise.

12 And tax-gatherers came also to be baptized, and they said to him, Teacher, what should we do?

13 And he said to them, Take no more [money] than what is appointed to you.

14 And persons engaged in military service also asked him saying, And we, what should we do? And he said to them, Oppress no one, nor accuse falsely, and be satisfied with your pay.

John Announces Masiah

15 But as the people were in expectation, and all were reasoning in their hearts concerning John whether he might be the Masiah,

16 John answered all, saying, I indeed baptize you with water, but the one coming is mightier than I, the thong of whose sandals I am not fit to unloose; he shall baptize you with the Holy Spirit and fire;

17 whose winnowing-fan is in his hand, and he will thoroughly purge his threshing-floor, and will gather the

wheat into his garner, but the chaff he
will burn with fire unquenchable.

18 Exhorting then many other things
also he announced [his] good news to
the people.

———————————————

Yehoshua Begins Ministry

Yehoshua about 30 Years of Age

Yehoshua is Water Baptized

Matt 3:13 Then comes Yehoshua from Galilee to the Jordan to John, to be baptized of him;

14 but John urgently forbade him, saying, I have need to be baptized of you; and you come to me?

15 But Yehoshua answering said to him, Permit [it] now; for thus it becomes us to fulfil all righteousness. Then he permits him.

16 And Yehoshua, having been baptized, went up straightway from the water, and lo, the heavens were opened to him, and he saw the Spirit of the God descending as a dove, and coming upon him:

17 and behold, a voice out of the heavens saying, This is my beloved Son, in whom I have found my delight.

Luke 3:23 And Yehoshua himself was beginning to be about of years thirty;

Devil Attempts to Tempt Yehoshua

Matt 4:1 Then Yehoshua was carried up into the wilderness by the Spirit to be tempted of the evil mind [daemon]

2 and having fasted forty days and forty nights, afterwards he hungered.

3 And the tempter coming up to him said, If you be Son of the God, speak, that these stones may become loaves of bread.

4 But he answering said, It is written, Man shall not live by bread alone, but by every word which goes out through God's mouth.

5 Then the evil mind [daemon] takes him to the holy city, and sets him upon the edge of the temple,

6 and says to him, If you be Son of the God cast thyself down; for it is written, He shall give charge to his angels concerning you, and on [their] hands shall they bear you, lest in anyway you strike your foot against a stone.

7 Yehoshua said to him, It is again written, You shall not tempt the Lord the God of you.

8 Again the evil mind [daemon] takes him to a very high mountain, and shows him all the kingdoms of the world, and their glory,

9 and says to him, All these things will I give you if, falling down, you will do me homage.

10 Then says Yehoshua to him, Get you away, Satan, for it is written, You shall do homage to the Lord the God of you, and him alone shall you serve.

11 Then the evil mind [daemon] leaves him, and behold, angels came and ministered to him.

John Explains his Ministry to Jerusalem Priests

John 1:19 And this is the witness of John, when the Jews sent from Jerusalem priests and Levites that they might ask him, Who are you?

20 And he acknowledged and denied not, and acknowledged, I am not the Masiah.

21 And they asked him, What then? Are you Elijah? And he says, I am not. Are you the prophet? And he answered, No.

22 They said therefore to him, Who are you? that we may give an answer to those who sent us. What do you say of yourself?

23 He said, I am the voice of one crying in the wilderness, Make straight the

path of the Lord, as Isaiah the prophet said.

24 And they were sent from among the Pharisees.

25 And they asked him and said to him, Why do you baptize then, if you are not the Masiah, nor Elijah, nor the prophet?

26 John answered them saying, I baptize with water. In the midst of you stands, whom you do not know,

27 he who comes after me, the thong of whose sandal I am not worthy to unloose.

28 These things took place in Bethany, across the Jordan, where John was baptizing.

John Proclaims Yehoshua Baptizes with Spirit and is the Lamb of God

29 On the next day he sees Yehoshua coming to him, and says, Behold the Lamb of the God, who takes away the sin of the world.

30 He it is of whom I said, A man comes after me who takes a place before me, because he was before me;

31 and I knew him not; but that he might be manifested to Israel, therefore have I come baptizing with water.

32 And John bore witness, saying, I beheld the Spirit descending as a dove from heaven, and it abode upon him.

33 And I knew him not; but he who sent me to baptize with water, he said to me, Upon whom you shall see the Spirit descending and abiding on him, he it is who baptizes with the Holy Spirit.

34 And I have seen and borne witness that this is the Son of the God.

35 Again, on the next day, there stood John and two of his disciples.

36 And, looking at Yehoshua as he walked, he says, Behold the Lamb of the God.

37 And the two disciples heard him speaking, and followed Yehoshua.

38 But Yehoshua having turned, and seeing them following, says to them, What do you seek? And they said to him, Rabbi which, being interpreted, signifies Teacher, where do you abide?

39 He says to them, Come and see. They went therefore, and saw where he abode; and they abode with him that day. It was about the tenth hour.

Apostles find and follow the Messiah

40 Andrew, the brother of Simon Peter, was one of the two who heard [this] from John and followed him.

41 He first finds his own brother Simon, and says to him, We have found the Messiah [which being interpreted is Christ].

42 And he led him to Yehoshua. Yehoshua looking at him said, You are Simon, the son of Jonas; you shall be called Cephas which interpreted is stone.

43 On the next day he would go forth into Galilee, and Yehoshua finds Philip, and says to him, Follow me.

44 And Philip was from Bethsaida, of the city of Andrew and Peter.

45 Philip finds Nathanael, and says to him, We have found him of whom Moses wrote in the law, and the prophets, Yehoshua, the son of Joseph, who is from Nazareth.

46 And Nathanael said to him, Can anything good come out of Nazareth? Philip says to him, Come and see.

47 Yehoshua saw Nathanael coming to him, and says of him, Behold [one] truly an Israelite, in whom there is no guile.

48 Nathanael says to him, From where do you know me? Yehoshua answered and said to him, Before that Philip called you, when you were under the fig-tree, I saw you.

49 Nathanael answered and said to him, Rabbi, you are the Son of the God, you are the King of Israel.

50 Yehoshua answered and said to him, Because I said to you, I saw you under the fig-tree, you believed? You shall see greater things than these.

51 And he says to him, Truly, truly, I say to you, Henceforth you shall see the heaven opened, and the angels of the God ascending and descending on the Son of man.

Yehoshua turns Water into Wine

John 2:1 And on the third day a marriage took place in Cana of Galilee, and the mother of Yehoshua was there.

2 And Yehoshua also, and his disciples, were invited to the marriage.

3 And wine being deficient, the mother of Yehoshua says to him, They have no wine.

4 Yehoshua says to her, What have I to do with you, woman? mine hour has not yet come.

5 His mother says to the servants, Whatever he may say to you, do.

6 Now there were standing there six stone water-vessels, according to the purification of the Jews, holding two or three measures each.

7 Yehoshua says to them, Fill the water-vessels with water. And they filled them up to the brim.

8 And he says to them, Draw out now, and carry [it] to the feast-master. And they carried [it]

9 But when the feast-master had tasted the water which had been made wine and knew not from where it was from, but the servants knew who drew the water, the feast-master calls the bridegroom,

10 and says to him, Every man sets out first the good wine, and when [men] have well drunk, then the inferior; you have kept the good wine till now.

11 This beginning of signs did Yehoshua in Cana of Galilee, and manifested his glory; and his disciples believed on him.

12 After this he descended to Capernaum, he and his mother and his brethren and his disciples; and there they abode not many days.

_____

First Passover of Yehoshua's Ministry

Yehoshua Drives Merchants from Temple

13 And the Passover[12] of the Jews was near, and Yehoshua went up to Jerusalem.

14 And he found in the temple the sellers of oxen and sheep and doves, and the money-changers sitting;

15 and, having made a scourge of cords, he cast [them] all out of the temple, both the sheep and the oxen; and he poured out the change of the money-changers, and overturned the tables,

16 and said to the sellers of doves, Take these things away; make not my Father's house a house of merchandise.

17 [And] his disciples remembered that it is written, The zeal of your house devours me.

Yehoshua: "Destroy this Temple..."

18 The Jews therefore answered and said to him, What sign will you show to us, that you do these things?

19 Yehoshua answered and said to them, Destroy this temple, and in three days I will raise it up.

20 The Jews therefore said, It took forty and six years for this temple to be built, and you will raise it up in three days?

21 But he spoke of the temple of his body.

22 When therefore he was raised from among the dead, his disciples remembered that he had said this, and believed the scripture and the word which Yehoshua had spoken.

23 And when he was in Jerusalem, at the Passover, at the feast, many believed on his name, beholding his signs which he worked.

24 But Yehoshua himself did not trust himself to them, because he knew all [men]

25 and that he had not need that any should testify of man, for himself knew what was in man.

Man Must be Born Again

John 3:1 But there was a man from among the Pharisees, his name Nicodemus, a ruler of the Jews;

2 he came to him by night, and said to him, Rabbi, we know that you are come a teacher from God, for none can do these signs that you do unless the God be with him.

3 Yehoshua answered and said to him, Truly, truly, I say unto you, Except any one be born anew he cannot see the kingdom of the God.

4 Nicodemus says to him, How can a man be born being old? can he enter a second time into the womb of his mother and be born?

5 Yehoshua answered, Truly, truly, I say unto you, Except any one be born of water and of Spirit, he cannot enter into the kingdom of the God.

6 That which is born of the flesh is flesh; and that which is born of the Spirit is spirit.

7 Do not wonder that I said to you, It is needful that you should be born anew.

8 The wind blows where it will, and you hear its voice, but know not from where it comes and where it goes: thus is every one that is born of the Spirit.

9 Nicodemus answered and said to him, How can these things be?

10 Yehoshua answered and said to him, You are the teacher of Israel and know not these things!

---

[12] First Passover of Ministry

11 Truly, truly, I say unto you, We speak that which we know, and we bear witness of that which we have seen, and you receive not our witness.

12 If I have said the earthly things to you, and you believe not, how, if I say the heavenly things to you, will you believe?

13 And no one has gone up into heaven, except he who came down* out of heaven, the Son of man [who is in heaven].

14 And as Moses lifted up the serpent in the wilderness, thus must the Son of man be lifted up,

15 that every one who believes on him may [not perish, but] have aeonian life.

16 For the God so loved the world, that he gave his one-of-a-kind[13] Son, that whosoever believes on him may not perish, but have aeonian life.

17 For the God has not sent his Son into the world that he may judge the world, but that the world may be saved through him.

18 He that believes on him is not judged: but he that believes not has been already judged, because he has not believed on the name of the one-of-a-kind[14] Son of the God.

19 And this is the judgment, that light is come into the world, and men have loved darkness rather than light; for their works were evil.

20 For every one that does evil hates the light, and does not come to the light that his works may not be shown as they are;

21 but he that practice the truth comes to the light, that his works may be manifested that they have been worked in God.

22 After these things came Yehoshua and his disciples into the land of Judea; and there he abode with them and baptized.

John the Baptist and Yehoshua

23 And John also was baptizing in Aenon, near Salim, because there was a great deal of water there; and they came to him and were baptized:

24 for John was not yet cast into prison.

25 There was therefore a reasoning of the disciples of John with a Jew about purification.

26 And they came to John and said to him, Rabbi, he who was with you beyond the Jordan, to whom you bore witness, behold, he baptizes, and all come to him.

27 John answered and said, A man can receive nothing unless it be given him out of heaven.

28 You yourselves bear me witness that I said, I am not the Masiah, but, that I am sent before him.

29 He that has the bride is the bridegroom; but the friend of the bridegroom, who stands and hears him, rejoices in heart because of the voice of the bridegroom: this my joy then is fulfilled.

30 He must increase, but I must decrease.

31 He who comes from above is above all. He who has his origin in the earth is of the earth, and speaks [as] of the earth. He who comes out of heaven is above all,

32 [and] what he has seen and has heard, this he testifies; and no one receives his testimony.

33 He that has received his testimony has set to his seal that the God is true;

34 for he whom the God has sent speaks the words of the God, for the God gives not the Spirit by measure [to him].

---

[13] GK: *monogenes*

[14] GK: *monogenes*

35 The Father loves the Son, and has given all things [to be] in his hand.

36 He that believes on the Son has aeonian life, and he that is not subject to the Son shall not see life, but the wrath of the God abides upon him.

Yehoshua Leaves Judea and goes to Galilee

John 4:1 When therefore the Lord knew that the Pharisees had heard that Yehoshua makes and baptizes more disciples than John

2 however, Yehoshua himself did not baptize, but his disciples,

3 he left Judea and went away again unto Galilee.

Yehoshua and the Samaritan Woman at the Well

4 And he had to pass through Samaria.

5 He comes therefore to a city of Samaria called Sychar, near to the land which Jacob gave to his son Joseph.

6 Now a fountain of Jacob's was there; Yehoshua therefore, being wearied with the way he had come, sat just as he was at the fountain. It was about the sixth hour.

7 A woman comes out of Samaria to draw water. Yehoshua says to her, Give me to drink

8 for his disciples had gone away into the city that they might buy provisions.

9 The Samaritan woman therefore says to him, How do you, being a Jew, ask to drink of me who am a Samaritan woman? for Jews have no intercourse with Samaritans.

10 Yehoshua answered and said to her, If you knew the gift of the God, and who it is that says to you, Give me to drink, you would have asked of him, and he would have given you living water.

11 The woman says to him, Sir, you have nothing to draw with, and the well is deep: from where do you get the living water?

12 Are you greater than our father Jacob, who gave us the well, and drank of it himself, and his sons, and his cattle?

13 Yehoshua answered and said to her, Every one who drinks of this water shall thirst again;

14 but whosoever drinks of the water which I shall give him shall never thirst into the aeon, but the water which I shall give him shall become in him a fountain of water, springing up into aeonian life.

15 The woman says to him, Sir, give me this water, that I may not thirst nor come here to draw.

16 Yehoshua says to her, Go, call your husband, and come here.

17 The woman answered and said, I have not a husband. Yehoshua says to her, You have well said, I have not a husband;

18 for you have had five husbands, and he whom now you have is not your husband: this you have spoken truly.

19 The woman says to him, Sir, I see that you are a prophet.

20 Our fathers worshiped in this mountain, and you say that in Jerusalem is the place where one must worship.

21 Yehoshua says to her, Woman, believe me, the hour is coming when you shall neither in this mountain nor in Jerusalem worship the Father.

22 You worship you know not what; we worship what we know, for salvation is of the Jews.

23 But the hour is coming and now is, when the true worshipers shall worship the Father in spirit and truth; for also the Father seeks such as his worshipers.

Yehoshua: "God [is] Spirit"

24 the God [is] spirit; and they who worship him must worship him in spirit and truth.

25 The woman says to him, I know that the Messiah is coming, who is called Christ; when he comes he will tell us all things.

26 Yehoshua says to her, I who speak to you am he.

27 And upon this came his disciples, and wondered that he spoke with a woman; yet no one said, What do you seek? or, Why speak you with her?

28 The woman then left her waterpot and went away into the city, and says to the men,

29 Come, see a man who told me all things I had ever done: is not he the Masiah?

30 They went out of the city and came to him.

Spiritual Food

31 But meanwhile the disciples asked him saying, Rabbi, eat.

32 But he said to them, I have food to eat which you do not know.

33 The disciples therefore said to one another, Has any one brought him [anything] to eat?

34 Yehoshua says to them, My food is that I should do the will of him that has sent me, and that I should finish his work.

35 Do not you say, that there are yet four months and the harvest comes? Behold, I say to you, Lift up your eyes and behold the fields, for they are already white to harvest.

36 He that reaps receives wages and gathers fruit unto aeonian life, that both he that sows and he that reaps may rejoice together.

37 For in this is [verified] the true saying, It is one who sows and another who reaps.

38 I have sent you to reap that on which you have not labored; others have labored, and you have entered into their labors.

39 But many of the Samaritans of that city believed on him because of the word of the woman who bore witness, He told me all things that I had ever done.

40 When therefore the Samaritans came to him they asked him to abide with them, and he abode there two days.

41 And more a great deal believed on account of his word;

42 and they said to the woman, [it is] no longer on account of your saying that we believe, for we have heard him ourselves, and we know that this is indeed the Savior of the world.

Yehoshua Continues onto Galilee

43 But after the two days he went forth from there and went away into Galilee,

44 for Yehoshua himself bore witness that a prophet has no honor in his own country.

45 When therefore he came into Galilee, the Galileans received him, having seen all that he had done in Jerusalem during the feast, for they also went to the feast.

Yehoshua Heals Boy in Capernaum

46 He came therefore again to Cana of Galilee, where he made the water wine. And there was a certain nobleman in Capernaum whose son was sick.

47 He, having heard that Yehoshua had come out of Judea into Galilee, went to him and asked him that he would come down and heal his son, for he was about to die.

48 Yehoshua therefore said to him, Unless you see signs and wonders you will not believe.

49 The nobleman says to him, Sir, come down else my child die.

50 Yehoshua says to him, Go, your son lives. And the man believed the word which Yehoshua said to him, and went his way.

51 But already, as he was going down, his servants met him and brought him word saying, Your child lives.

52 He inquired therefore from them the hour at which he got better. And they said to him, Yesterday at the seventh hour the fever left him.

53 The father therefore knew that [it was] in that hour in which Yehoshua said to him, Your son lives; and he believed, himself and his whole house.

54 This was the second sign that Yehoshua did since coming out of Judea into Galilee.

John the Baptist Imprisoned

Luke 3:19 But Herod the tetrarch, being reproved by him as to Herodias, the wife of his brother, and as to all the wicked things which Herod had done,

20 added this also to all [the rest] that he shut up John in prison.

Yehoshua teaches about the Coming of the Kingdom

Matt 4:12 But having heard that John was delivered up, he departed into Galilee:

13 and having left Nazareth, he went and dwelt at Capernaum, which is on the sea-side in the borders of Zabulon and Nepthalim,

14 that that might be fulfilled which was spoken through Isaiah the prophet, saying,

> 15 Land of Zabulon and land of Nepthalim, way of the sea beyond the Jordan, Galilee of the nations:

> 16 --the people sitting in darkness has seen a great light, and to those sitting in the country and shadow of death, to them has light sprung up.

17 From that time began Yehoshua to preach and to say, Repent, for the kingdom of the heavens has drawn near.

Luke 4:14 And Yehoshua returned in the power of the Spirit to Galilee; and a rumor went out into the whole surrounding country about him;

15 and he taught in their synagogues, being glorified of all.

Yehoshua Announces His Mission

16 And he came to Nazareth, where he was brought up; and he entered, according to his custom, into the synagogue on the sabbaths, and stood up to read.

17 [And] the book of the prophet Isaiah was given to him; and having unrolled the book he found the place where it was written,

18 the Spirit of the Lord is upon me, because he has anointed me to preach good news to the poor; he has sent me to preach to captives deliverance, and to the blind sight, to send forth the crushed delivered,

19 to preach the acceptable year of the Lord.

20 And having rolled up the book, when he had delivered it up to the attendant, he sat down; and the eyes of all in the synagogue were fixed upon him.

21 And he began to say to them, Today this scripture is fulfilled in your ears.

22 And all bore witness to him, and wondered at the words of grace which were coming out of his mouth. And they said, Is not this the son of Joseph?

No Prophet is Accepted in his own Country

23 And he said to them, You will surely say to me this parable, Physician, heal yourself; whatsoever we have heard has taken place in Capernaum do here also in your own country.

24 And he said, Truly I say to you, that no prophet is acceptable in his [own] country.

Few Miracles

25 But of a truth I say to you, There were many widows in Israel in the days of Elijah, when the heaven was shut up for three years and six months, so that a great famine came upon all the land,

26 and to none of them was Elijah sent but to Sarepta of Sidonia, to a woman [that was] a widow.

27 And there were many lepers in Israel in the time of Elisha the prophet, and none of them was cleansed but Naaman the Syrian.

Yehoshua Rejected

28 And they were all filled with rage in the synagogue, hearing these things;

29 and rising up they cast him forth out of the city, and led him up to the brow of the mountain upon which their city was built, so that they might throw him down the precipice;

30 but he, passing through the midst of them, went his way,

Yehoshua Teaches on the Sabbath

31 and descended to Capernaum, a city of Galilee, and taught them on the sabbaths.

32 And they were astonished at his doctrine, for his word was with authority.

Yehoshua Casts Out Daemon

33 And there was in the synagogue a man having a spirit of an unclean daemon, and he cried with a loud voice,

34 saying, Eh! what have we to do with you, Yehoshua, Nazarene? have you come to destroy us? I know you who you are, the Holy [one] of the God.

35 And Yehoshua rebuked him, saying, Hold your peace, and come out from him. And the daemon, having thrown him down into the midst, came out from him without doing him any injury.

36 And astonishment came upon all, and they spoke to one another, saying,

What word [is] this? for with authority and power he commands the unclean spirits, and they come out.

37 And a rumor went out into every place of the country round concerning him.

Yehoshua Heals Simon's Mother-in-law

38 And rising up out of the synagogue, he entered into the house of Simon. But Simon's mother-in-law was suffering under a bad fever; and they asked him for her.

39 And standing over her, he rebuked the fever, and it left her; and forthwith standing up she served them.

At Sundown Yehoshua Heals the Sick

40 And when the sun went down, all, as many as had persons sick with diverse diseases, brought them to him, and having laid his hands on every one of them, he healed them;

Daemons Call Yehoshua, "Son of God"

41 and daemons also went out from many, crying out and saying, You are the Son of the God. And rebuking them, he permitted them not to speak, because they knew him to be the Masiah.

Yehoshua Teaches the Good News

42 And when it was day he went out, and went into a desolate place, and the crowds sought after him, and came up to him, and [would have] kept him back that he should not go from them.

43 But he said to them, I must needs announce the good news of the kingdom of the God to the other cities also, for this I have been sent forth.

44 And he was preaching in the synagogues of Galilee.

Huge Catch of Fish at Lake Gennesaret

Luke 5:1 And it came to pass, as the crowd pressed on him to hear the word of the God, that he was standing by the lake of Gennesaret:

2 and he saw two ships standing by the lake, but the fishermen, having come down from them, were washing their nets.

3 And getting into one of the ships, which was Simon's, he asked him to draw out a little from the land; and he sat down and taught the crowds out of the ship.

4 But when he ceased speaking, he said to Simon, Draw out into the deep [water] and let down your nets for a haul.

5 And Simon answering said to him, Master, having labored through the whole night we have taken nothing, but at your word I will let down the net.

6 And having done this, they enclosed a great multitude of fishes. And their net broke.

7 And they beckoned to their partners who were in the other ship to come and help them, and they came, and filled both the ships, so that they were sinking.

8 But Simon Peter, seeing it, fell at Yehoshua's knees, saying, Depart from me, for I am a sinful man, Lord.

9 For astonishment had laid hold on him, and on all those who were with him, at the haul of fishes which they had taken;

10 and in like manner also on James and John, sons of Zebedee, who were partners with Simon. And Yehoshua said to Simon, Fear not, henceforth you shall be fishers of men.

Simon, Andrew, James, and John

Matt 4:18 And walking by the sea of Galilee, he saw two brothers, Simon called Peter, and Andrew his brother, casting a net into the sea, for they were fishermen;

19 and he says to them, Come after me, and I will make you fishermen of men.

20 And they, having left their trawl-nets, immediately followed him.

21 And going on from there he saw other two brothers, James the [son] of Zebedee and John his brother, in the ship with Zebedee their father, mending their trawl-nets, and he called them;

22 and they, having left the ship and their father, immediately followed him.

Yehoshua Teaches and Heals at Capernaum

Mark 1:21 And they go into Capernaum. And straightway on the Sabbath he entered into the synagogue and taught.

22 And they were astonished at his doctrine, for he taught them as having authority, and not as the scribes.

23 And there was in their synagogue a man [possessed] by an unclean spirit, and he cried out,

24 saying, Eh! what have we to do with you, Yehoshua, Nazarene? Are you come to destroy us? I know you who you are, the holy one of the God.

25 And Yehoshua rebuked him, saying, Hold thy peace and come out of him.

26 And the unclean spirit, having torn him, and uttered a cry with a loud voice, came out of him.

27 And all were amazed, so that they questioned together among themselves, saying, What is this? what new doctrine is this? for with authority he commands even the unclean spirits, and they obey him.

28 And his fame went out straightway into the whole region of Galilee around.

29 And straightway going out of the synagogue, they came with James and John into the house of Simon and Andrew.

30 And the mother-in-law of Simon lay in a fever. And straightway they speak to him about her.

31 And he went up to [her] and raised her up, having taken her by the hand, and straightway the fever left her, and she served them.

32 But evening being come, when the sun had gone down, they brought to him all that were suffering, and those possessed by demons;

33 and the whole city was gathered together at the door.

34 And he healed many suffering from various diseases; and he cast out many daemons, and did not permit the daemons to speak because they knew him.

35 And rising in the morning long before day, he went out and went away into a desolate place, and there prayed.

36 And Simon and those with him went after him:

37 and having found him, they say to him, All seek you.

38 And he says to them, Let us go elsewhere into the neighboring country towns, that I may preach there also, for this purpose I have come forth.

39 And he was preaching in their synagogues in the whole of Galilee, and casting out daemons.

Yehoshua Travels about Galilee Teaching

Matt 4:23 And [Yehoshua] went round the whole of Galilee, teaching in their synagogues, and preaching the good news of the kingdom, and healing every disease and every bodily weakness among the people.

24 And his fame went out into the whole of Syria, and they brought to him all that were ill, suffering under various diseases and pains, and those possessed by daemons, and lunatics, and paralytics; and he healed them.

25 And great crowds followed him from Galilee, and Decapolis, and Jerusalem, and Judea, and beyond the Jordan.

Miracles

Mark 1:40 And there comes to him a leper, beseeching him, and falling on his knees to him, and saying to him, If you will you can cleanse me.

41 But Yehoshua, moved with compassion, having stretched out his hand, touched him, and says to him, I will, be you cleansed.

42 And as he spoke straightway the leprosy left him, and he was cleansed.

43 And having sharply charged him, he straightway sent him away,

44 and says to him, See you say nothing to any one, but go, show yourself to the priest, and offer for your cleansing what Moses ordained, for a testimony to them.

45 But he, having gone forth, began to proclaim [it] much, and to spread the matter abroad, so that he could no longer enter openly into the city, but was outside in desolate places, and they came to him from every side.

Mark 2:1 And he entered again into Capernaum after [several] days, and it was reported that he was at the house;

2 and straightway many were gathered together, so that there was no longer any room, not even at the door; and he spoke the word to them.

3 And there come to him [men] bringing a paralytic, borne by four;

4 and, not being able to get near to him on account of the crowd, they uncovered the roof where he was, and having dug [it] up they let down the couch on which the paralytic lay.

5 But Yehoshua, seeing their faith, says to the paralytic, Child, your sins are forgiven [you]

Scribes Question Yehoshua's Authority

6 But certain of the scribes were there sitting, and reasoning in their hearts,

7 Why does this [man] thus speak? he blasphemes. Who is able to forgive sins except the God alone?

8 And straightway Yehoshua, knowing in his spirit that they are reasoning thus within themselves, said to them, Why reason you these things in your hearts?

9 Which is easier, to say to the paralytic, [your] sins are forgiven [you] or to say, Arise, and take up your couch and walk?

10 But that you may know that the Son of man has power on earth to forgive sins, he says to the paralytic,

11 To you I say, Arise, take up your couch and go to your house.

12 And he rose up straightway, and, having taken up his couch, went out before [them] all, so that all were amazed, and glorified the God, saying, We never saw it thus.

Matthew (Levi) is Called

13 And he went out again by the sea, and all the crowd came to him, and he taught them.

14 And passing by, he saw Levi the [son] of Alphaeus sitting at the tax-office, and says to him, Follow me. And he rose up and followed him.

Eating with Sinners

Matt 9:10 And it came to pass, as he lay at table in the house, that behold, many tax-gatherers and sinners came and lay at table with Yehoshua and his disciples.

11 And the Pharisees seeing [it] said to his disciples, Why does your teacher eat with tax-gatherers and sinners?

12 But [Yehoshua] hearing it, said, They that are strong have not need of a physician, but those that are ill.

13 But go and learn what that is – I will have mercy and not sacrifice; for I have not come to call righteous [men] but sinners.

Questions about Disciples not Fasting

Luke 5:29 And Levi made a great entertainment for him in his house, and there was a great crowd of tax-gatherers and others who were at table with them.

30 And their scribes and the Pharisees murmured at his disciples, saying, Why do you eat and drink with tax-gatherers and sinners?

31 And Yehoshua answering said to them, They that are in sound health have not need of a physician, but those that are ill.

32 I am not come to call righteous [persons] but sinful [ones] to repentance

33 And they said to him, Why do the disciples of John fast often and make supplications, in like manner those also of the Pharisees, but you eat and drink?

34 And he said to them, Can you make the sons of the bride chamber fast when the bridegroom is with them?

35 But days will come when also the bridegroom will have been taken away from them; then shall they fast in those days.

36 And he spoke also a parable to them: No one puts a piece of a new garment upon an old garment, otherwise he will both rip the new, and the piece which is from the new will not suit with the old.

37 And no one puts new wine into old skins, otherwise the new wine will burst the skins, and it will be poured out, and the skins will be destroyed;

38 but new wine is to be put into new skins, and both are preserved.

39 And no one having drunk old wine [straightway] wishes for new, for he says, The old is better.

Second Passover of Yehoshua's Ministry

Yehoshua Back in Jerusalem: Healing at the Pool of Bethesda

John 5:1 After these things was a feast[15] of the Jews, and Yehoshua went up to Jerusalem.

2 Now there is in Jerusalem, at the sheepgate, a pool, which is called in Hebrew, Bethesda, having five porches.

3 In these lay a multitude of sick, blind, lame, withered, [awaiting the moving of the water.

4 For an angel descended at a certain season in the pool and troubled the water. Whoever therefore first went in after the troubling of the water became well, whatever disease he labored under]

5 But there was a certain man there who had been suffering under his infirmity thirty and eight years.

6 Yehoshua seeing this [man] lying [there] and knowing that he was [in that state] now a great length of time, says to him, Do you want to become well?

7 The infirm [man] answered him, Sir, I have not a man, in order, when the water has been troubled, to cast me into the pool; but while I am coming another descends before me.

8 Yehoshua says to him, Arise, take up your couch and walk.

Healing on Sabbath Questioned

9 And immediately the man became well, and took up his couch and walked: and on that day was Sabbath.

10 The Jews therefore said to the healed [man] It is Sabbath, it is not permitted you to take up your couch.

11 He answered them, He that made me well, he said to me, Take up your couch and walk.

12 They asked him [therefore] Who is the man who said to you, Take up your couch and walk?

13 But he that had been healed knew not who it was, for Yehoshua had slid away, there being a crowd in the place.

14 After these things Yehoshua finds him in the temple, and said to him, Behold, you are become well: sin no more, that something worse do not happen to you.

15 The man went away and told the Jews that it was Yehoshua who had made him well.

Resurrection and Life

16 And for this the Jews persecuted Yehoshua [and sought to kill him] because he had done these things on Sabbath.

17 But Yehoshua answered them, My Father works until now, and I work.

18 For this therefore the Jews sought the more to kill him, because he had not only violated the Sabbath, but also said that the God was his own Father, making himself equal with God.

19 Yehoshua therefore answered and said to them, Truly, truly, I say to you, The Son can do nothing of himself except whatever he sees the Father doing: for whatever things he does, these things also the Son does in like manner.

20 For the Father loves the Son and shows him all things which he himself does; and he will show him greater works than these, that you may wonder.

21 For even as the Father raises the dead and gives life, thus the Son also gives life to whom he will:

---

[15] 2nd Passover of Ministry

22 for neither does the Father judge any one, but has given all judgment to the Son;

23 that all may honor the Son, even as they honor the Father. He who honors not the Son, honors not the Father who has sent him.

24 Truly, truly, I say unto you, that he that hears my word, and believes him that has sent me, has aeonian life, and does not come into judgment, but is passed out of death into life.

25 Truly, truly, I say unto you, that an hour is coming, and now is, when the dead shall hear the voice of the Son of the God, and they that have heard shall live.

26 For even as the Father has life in himself, so he has given to the Son also to have life in himself,

27 and has given him authority to execute judgment [also] because he is Son of man.

28 Wonder not at this, for an hour is coming in which all who are in the tombs shall hear his voice,

29 and shall go forth; those that have practiced good, to resurrection of life, and those that have done evil, to resurrection of judgment.

Yehoshua's Authority

30 I cannot do anything of myself; as I hear, I judge, and my judgment is righteous, because I do not seek my will, but the will of him that has sent me.

31 If I bear witness concerning myself, my witness is not true.

32 It is another who bears witness concerning me, and I know that the witness which he bears concerning me is true.

33 You have sent unto John, and he has borne witness to the truth.

34 But I do not receive witness from man, but I say this that you might be saved.

35 He was the burning and shining lamp, and you were willing for a season to rejoice in his light.

36 But I have the witness [that is] greater than that of John; for the works which the Father has given me that I should complete them, the works themselves which I do, bear witness concerning me that the Father has sent me.

37 And the Father who has sent me himself has borne witness concerning me. You have neither heard his voice at any time, nor have seen his shape,

38 and you have not his word abiding in you; for whom he hath sent, him you do not believe.

39 You search the scriptures, for you think that in them you have aeonian life, and they it is which bear witness concerning me;

40 and you will not come to me that you might have life.

41 I do not receive glory from men,

42 but I know you, that you have not the love of the God in you.

43 I am come in my Father's name, and you accept me not; if another come in his own name, him you will accept.

44 How can you believe, who receive glory one of another, and seek not the glory which [comes] from the God alone?

45 Think not that I will accuse you to the Father: there is [one] who accuses you, Moses, on whom you trust;

46 for if you had believed Moses, you would have believed me, for he wrote of me.

47 But if you do not believe his writings, how shall you believe my words?

Picking Grain on the Sabbath

Matt 12:1 At that time Yehoshua went on the sabbaths through the grainfields; and his disciples were hungry, and began to pluck the ears and to eat.

2 But the Pharisees, seeing [it] said to him, Behold, your disciples are doing what is not lawful to do on sabbaths.

3 But he said to them, Have you not read what David did when he was hungry, and they that were with him?

4 How he entered into the house of the God, and ate the showbread, which it was not lawful for him to eat, nor for those with him, but for the priests only?

5 Or have you not read in the law that on the sabbaths the priests in the temple profane the Sabbath, and are blameless?

6 But I say unto you, that there is here what is greater than the temple.

7 But if you had known what this means: I wish for mercy and not sacrifice, you would not have condemned the guiltless.

8 For the Son of man is Lord of the Sabbath.

[Mark 2:23 And it came to pass that he went on the sabbaths through the grainfields; and his disciples began to walk on, plucking the ears.

24 And the Pharisees said to him, Behold, why do they on the sabbaths what is not lawful?

25 And he said to them, Have you never read what David did when he had need and hungered, he and those with him,

26 how he entered into the house of the God, in [the section of] Abiathar the high priest, and ate the show-bread, which it is not lawful unless for the priests to eat, and gave even to those that were with him?

27 And he said to them, The Sabbath was made on account of man, not man on account of the Sabbath;

28 so that the Son of man is lord of the Sabbath also.]

Healing on the Sabbath

Matt 12:9 And, going away from there, he came into their synagogue.

10 And behold, there was a man having his hand withered. And they asked him, saying, Is it lawful to heal on the sabbaths? that they might accuse him.

11 But he said to them, What man shall there be of you who has one sheep, and if this fall into a pit on the sabbaths, will not lay hold of it and raise [it] up?

12 How much better then is a man than a sheep! So that it is lawful to do well on the sabbaths.

13 Then he says to the man, Stretch out your hand. And he stretched [it] out, and it was restored sound as the other.

14 But the Pharisees, having gone out, took counsel against him, how they might destroy him.

Yehoshua Continues to Heal

15 But Yehoshua knowing [it] withdrew from there, and great crowds followed him; and he healed them all:

16 and charged them strictly that they should not make him publicly known:

17 that that might be fulfilled which was spoken through Isaiah the prophet, saying,

18 Behold my servant, whom I have chosen, my beloved, in whom my soul has found its delight. I will put my Spirit upon him, and he shall show forth judgment to the nations.

19 He shall not strive or cry out, nor shall any one hear his voice in the streets;

20 a bruised reed shall he not break, and smoking flax shall he not quench,

until he bring forth judgment unto victory;

21 and on his name shall the nations hope.

> [Mark 3:7 And Yehoshua withdrew with his disciples to the sea; and a great multitude from Galilee followed him, and from Judea,
>
> 8 and from Jerusalem, and from Idumaea and beyond the Jordan; and they of around Tyre and Sidon, a great multitude, having heard what things he did, came to him.
>
> 9 And he spoke to his disciples, in order that a little ship should wait upon him on account of the crowd, that they might not press upon him.
>
> 10 For he healed many, so that they beset him that they might touch him, as many as had plagues.
>
> 11 And the unclean spirits, when they beheld him, fell down before him, and cried saying, You are the Son of the God.
>
> 12 And he rebuked them much, that they might not make him manifest.]

Yehoshua Chooses Twelve Apostles

Luke 6:12 And it came to pass in those days that he went out into the mountain to pray, and he spent the night in prayer to the God.

13 And when it was day he called his disciples, and having chosen out twelve from them, whom also he named apostles:

14 Simon, to whom also he gave the name of Peter, and Andrew his brother, [and] James and John, [and] Philip and Bartholomew,

15 [and] Matthew and Thomas, James the [son] of Alphaeus and Simon who was called Zealot,

16 [and] Judas [brother] of James, and Judas Iscariote, who was also [his] betrayer;

Great Crowd Gathers

17 and having descended with them, he stood on a level place, and a crowd of his disciples, and a great multitude of the people from all Judea and Jerusalem, and the sea coast of Tyre and Sidon, who came to hear him, and to be healed of their diseases;

18 and those that were beset by unclean spirits were healed.

19 And all the crowd sought to touch him, for power went out from him and healed all.

Sermon on the Mount

Matt 5:1 But seeing the crowds, he went up into the mountain, and having sat down, his disciples came to him;

2 and, having opened his mouth, he taught them, saying,

3 Blessed [are] the poor in spirit, for theirs is the kingdom of the heavens.

4 Blessed they that mourn, for they shall be comforted.

5 Blessed the meek, for they shall inherit the earth.

6 Blessed they who hunger and thirst after righteousness, for they shall be filled.

7 Blessed the merciful, for they shall find mercy.

8 Blessed the pure in heart, for they shall see the God.

9 Blessed the peace-makers, for they shall be called sons of God.

10 Blessed they who are persecuted on account of righteousness, for theirs is the kingdom of the heavens.

11 Blessed are you when they may reproach and persecute you, and say every wicked thing against you, lying, for my sake.

12 Rejoice and exult, for your reward is great in the heavens; for thus have they persecuted the prophets who were before you.

Luke 6:24 But woe to you rich, for you have received your consolation.

25 Woe to you that are filled, for you shall hunger. Woe to you who laugh now, for you shall mourn and weep.

26 Woe, when all men speak well of you, for after this manner did their fathers to the false prophets.

Salt of the Earth

Matt 5:13 You are the salt of the earth; but if the salt have become insipid, wherewith shall it be salted? It is no longer fit for anything but to be cast out and to be trodden under foot by men.

14 You are the light of the world: a city situated on the top of a mountain cannot be hid.

15 Nor do [men] light a lamp and put it under the bushel, but upon the lamp-stand, and it shines for all who are in the house.

16 Let your light thus shine before men, so that they may see your upright works, and glorify your Father who is in the heavens.

Law and Grace

17 Think not that I am come to make void the law or the prophets; I am not come to make void, but to fulfil.

18 For truly I say unto you, Until the heaven and the earth pass away, one iota or one tittle shall in no way pass from the law till all come to pass.

19 Whosoever then shall do away with one of these least commandments, and shall teach men so, shall be called least in the kingdom of the heavens; but whosoever shall practice and teach [them] he shall be called great in the kingdom of the heavens.

20 For I say unto you, that unless your righteousness surpass that of the scribes and Pharisees, you shall in no way enter into the kingdom of the heavens.

On Murder

21 You have heard that it was said to the ancients, You shall not kill; but whosoever shall kill shall be subject to the judgment.

22 But I say unto you, that every one that is angry with his brother shall be subject to the judgment; but whosoever shall say to his brother, Raca, shall be subject to [be called before] the Sanhedrim; but whosoever shall say, Fool, shall be subject to the penalty of the hell [Gehenna] of fire.

23 If therefore you should offer your gift at the altar, and there should remember that your brother has something against you,

24 leave there your gift before the altar, and first go, be reconciled to your brother, and then come and offer your gift.

Make Friends

25 Make friends with your adverse party quickly, while you are in the way with him; lest some time the adverse party deliver you to the judge, and the judge deliver you to the officer, and you be cast into prison.

26 Truly I say to you, You shall in no way come out from there till you have paid the last quarter [quadrans].

On Adultery

27 You have heard that it has been said, You shall not commit adultery.

28 But I say unto you, that every one who looks upon a woman to lust after her has already committed adultery with her in his heart.

Cut Off Your Hand ...

29 But if your right eye be a snare to you, pluck it out and cast it from you: for

it is profitable for you that one of your members perish, and not your whole body be cast into hell [Gehenna].

30 And if your right hand be a snare to you, cut it off and cast it from you: for it is profitable for you that one of your members perish, and not your whole body be cast into hell [Gehenna].

On Marriage and Divorce

31 It has been said too, Whosoever shall put away his wife, let him give her a letter of divorce.

32 But I say unto you, that whosoever shall put away his wife, except for cause of fornication, makes her commit adultery, and whosoever marries one that is put away commits adultery.

On Honesty without Oaths

33 Again, you have heard that it has been said to the ancients, You shall not forswear yourself, but shall render to the Lord what you have sworn.

34 But I say unto you, Do not swear at all; neither by the heaven, because it is the throne of the God;

35 nor by the earth, because it is the footstool of his feet; nor by Jerusalem, because it is the city of the great King.

36 Neither shall you swear by your head, because you can not make one hair white or black.

37 But let your word be Yes, yes; No, no; but what is more than these is from evil.

Golden Rule

38 You have heard that it has been said, Eye for eye and tooth for tooth.

39 But I say unto you, not to resist evil; but whoever shall strike you on your right cheek, turn to him also the other;

40 and to him that would go to law with you and take your body coat, leave him your cloak also.

41 And whoever will compel you to go one mile, go with him two.

42 To him that asks of you give, and from him that desires to borrow of you turn not away.

Luke 6:31 And as you wish that men should do to you, do you also to them in like manner.

Love for Enemies

43 You have heard that it has been said, You shall love your neighbor and hate your enemy.

44 But I say unto you, Love your enemies, [bless those who curse you] do good to those who hate you, and pray for those who [insult you and] persecute you,

45 that you may be the sons of your Father who is in the heavens; for he makes his sun rise on evil and good, and sends rain on just and unjust.

46 For if you should love those who love you, what reward have you? Do not also the tax-gatherers the same?

47 And if you should salute your brethren only, what do you extraordinary? Do not also the Gentiles the same?

48 Be you therefore perfect as your heavenly Father is perfect.

Luke 6:34 And if you lend to those from whom you hope to receive, what favor is it to you? [for] even sinners lend to sinners that they may receive the like.

35 But love your enemies, and do good, and lend, expecting nothing in return, and your reward shall be great, and you shall be sons of the Highest; for he is good to the unthankful and wicked.

36 Be you therefore merciful, even as your Father also is merciful.

On Giving

Matt 6:1 Take heed not to do your alms before men to be seen of them, otherwise you have no reward with your Father who is in the heavens.

2 When therefore you do alms, sound not a trumpet before you, as the hypocrites do in the synagogues and in the streets, so that they may have glory from men. Truly I say unto you, They have their reward.

3 But you, when you do alms, let not your left hand know what your right hand does;

4 so that your alms may be in secret, and your Father who sees in secret will render [it] to you.

On Praying

5 And when you pray, you shall not be as the hypocrites; for they like to pray standing in the synagogues and in the corners of the streets so that they should appear to men. Truly I say unto you, They have their reward.

6 But you, when you pray, enter into your chamber, and having shut your door, pray to your Father who is in secret, and your Father who sees in secret will render [it] to you.

7 But when you pray, use not vain repetitions, as those who are of the nations: for they think they shall be heard through their much speaking.

8 Be not you therefore like them, for your Father knows of what things you have need before you beg [anything] of him.

9 Thus therefore pray you: Our Father who are in the heavens, let your name be sanctified,

10 let your kingdom come, let your will be done as in heaven so upon the earth;

11 give us today our needed bread,

12 and forgive us our debts, as we also forgive our debtors,

13 and lead us not into temptation, but save us from evil.

14 For if you forgive men their offences, your heavenly Father also will forgive you [yours]

15 but if you do not forgive men their offences, neither will your Father forgive your offences.

On Fasting

16 And when you fast, be not as the hypocrites, downcast in countenance; for they disfigure their faces, so that they may appear fasting to men: truly I say unto you, They have their reward.

17 But you, [when] fasting, anoint your head and wash your face,

18 so that you may not appear fasting unto men, but to your Father who is in secret; and your Father who sees in secret shall render [it] to you.

Spiritual Treasures

19 Lay not up for yourselves treasures upon the earth, where moth and rust spoils, and where thieves dig through and steal;

20 but lay up for yourselves treasures in heaven, where neither moth nor rust spoils, and where thieves do not dig through nor steal;

21 for where your treasure is, there will be also your heart.

Light: Real and Dark

22 The lamp of the body is the eye; if therefore your eye be clear, your whole body will be light:

23 but if your eye be wicked, your whole body will be dark. If therefore the light that is in you be darkness, how great the darkness!

Cannot Serve Two Masters

24 No one can serve two masters; for either he will hate the one and will love the other, or he will hold to the one and despise the other. You cannot serve God and mammon.

On Anxiety

25 For this cause I say unto you, Do not be concerned about your soul, what you should eat and what you should drink; nor for your body what you should put

on. Is not the soul more than food, and the body than clothes?

26 Look at the birds of the heaven, that they sow not, nor reap, nor gather into granaries, and your heavenly Father nourishes them. Are you not much more excellent than they?

27 But which of you by concern can add to his growth one cubit?

28 And why are you concerned about clothing? Observe with attention the lilies of the field, how they grow: they toil not, neither do they spin;

29 but I say unto you, that not even Solomon in all his glory was clothed as one of these.

30 But if the God so clothe the herbage of the field, which is today, and tomorrow is cast into the oven, will he not much rather clothe you, O [you] of little faith?

31 Be not therefore concerned, saying, What shall we eat? or What shall we drink? or What shall we put on?

32 for all these things the nations seek after; for your heavenly Father knows that you have need of all these things.

33 But seek you first the kingdom of the God and his righteousness, and all these things shall be added unto you.

34 Be not concerned therefore for the tomorrow, for the tomorrow shall be concerned about itself. Sufficient to the day [is] its own evil.

Hypocritical Judging

Luke 6:37 And judge not, and you shall not be judged; condemn not, and you shall not be condemned. Forgive, and it shall be forgiven you.

38 Give, and it shall be given to you; good measure, pressed down, and shaken together, and running over, shall be given into your bosom: for with the same measure with which you measured it shall be measured to you again.

39 And he spoke also a parable to them: Can a blind [man] lead a blind [man]? shall not both fall into the ditch?

40 The disciple is not above his teacher, but every one that is perfected shall be as his teacher.

41 But why look you on the straw which is in the eye of your brother, but perceive not the beam which is in your own eye?

42 or how can you say to your brother, Brother, allow [me] I will cast out the straw that is in your eye, yourself not seeing the beam that is in your eye? Hypocrite, cast out first the beam out of your eye, and then you shall see clear to cast out the straw which is in the eye of your brother.

> [Matt 7:1 Judge not, that you may not be judged;
>
> 2 for with the judgment you judge, you shall be judged; and with what measure you measured, it shall be measured to you.
>
> 3 But why look you on the straw that is in the eye of your brother, but observe not the log that is in your eye?
>
> 4 Or how will you say to your brother, Allow [me] I will cast out the straw from your eye; and behold, the beam is in your eye?
>
> 5 Hypocrite, cast out first the beam out of your eye, and then you will see clearly to cast out the straw out of the eye of your brother.]

Don't Give Pearls to Swine or Holy Things to Dogs

Matt 7:6 Give not that which is holy to the dogs, nor cast your pearls before the swine, lest they trample them with their feet, and turning round rip you.

Seek and you shall find; Golden Rule

7 Ask, and it shall be given to you. Seek, and you shall find. Knock, and it shall be opened to you.

8 For every one that asks receives; and he that seeks finds; and to him that knocks it shall be opened.

9 Or what man is there of you who, if his son shall ask of him a loaf of bread, will give him a stone;

10 and if he ask a fish, will give him a serpent?

11 If therefore you, being wicked, know [how] to give good gifts to your children, how much rather shall your Father who is in the heavens give good things to them that ask of him?

12 Therefore all things whatever you desire that men should do to you, thus do you also do to them; for this is the [meaning of the] law and the prophets.

Narrow Gate

13 Enter in through the narrow gate, for wide the gate and broad the way that leads to destruction, and many are they who enter in through it.

14 For narrow the gate and straitened the way that leads to life, and they are few who find it.

False Prophets, By their Fruit you shall know them

15 But beware of false prophets, which come to you in sheep's clothing, but within are ravening wolves.

16 By their fruits you shall know them. Do [men] gather a bunch of grapes from thorns, or from thistles figs?

17 So every good tree produces good fruits, but the worthless tree produces bad fruits.

18 A good tree cannot produce bad fruits, nor a worthless tree produce good fruits.

19 Every tree not producing good fruit is cut down and cast into the fire.

20 By their fruits then surely you shall know them.

Luke 6:43 For there is no good tree which produces corrupt fruit, nor a corrupt tree which produces good fruit;

44 for every tree is known by its own fruit, for figs are not gathered from thorns, nor grapes vintaged from a bramble.

45 The good man, out of the good treasure of his heart, brings forth good; and the wicked [man] out of the wicked, brings forth what is wicked: for out of the abundance of the heart his mouth speaks.

Not Every One Who Says "Lord, Lord" ...

Matt 7:21 Not every one who says to me, Lord, Lord, shall enter into the kingdom of the heavens, but he that does the will of my Father who is in the heavens.

22 Many shall say to me in that day, Lord, Lord, have we not prophesied through your name, and through your name cast out daemons, and through your name done many works of power?

23 and then will I avow unto them, I never knew you. Depart from me, workers of lawlessness.

Words and Deeds

Luke 6:46 And why call you me, Lord, Lord, and do not the things that I say?

Matt 7:24 Whoever therefore hears these my words and does them, I will liken him to a prudent man, who built his house upon the rock;

25 and the rain came down, and the streams came, and the winds blew and fell upon that house, and it did not fall, for it had been founded upon the rock.

26 And every one who hears these my words and does not do them, he shall be likened to a foolish man, who built his house upon the sand;

27 and the rain came down, and the streams came, and the winds blew and beat upon that house, and it fell, and its fall was great.

Crowds Astonished

28 And it came to pass, when Yehoshua had finished these words, the crowds were astonished at his doctrine,

29 for he taught them as having authority, and not as their scribes.

Centurion's Slave Healed

Luke 7:1 And when he had completed all his words in the hearing of the people, he entered into Capernaum.

2 And a certain centurion's servant who was dear to him was ill and about to die;

3 and having heard of Yehoshua, he sent to him elders of the Jews, begging him that he might come and save his servant.

4 But they, being come to Yehoshua, besought him diligently, saying, He is worthy to whom you should grant this,

5 for he loves our nation, and himself has built the synagogue for us.

6 And Yehoshua went with them. But already, when he was not far from the house, the centurion sent to him friends, saying to him, Lord, do not trouble yourself, for I am not worthy that you should enter under my roof.

7 Wherefore neither did I count myself worthy to come to you. But say by a word and my servant shall be healed.

8 For I also am a man placed under authority, having under myself soldiers, and I say to this [one] Go, and he goes; and to another, Come, and he comes; and to my servant, Do this, and he does [it]

9 And Yehoshua hearing this wondered at him, and turning to the crowd following him said, I say to you, Not even in Israel have I found so great faith.

Matt 8:11 But I say unto you, that many shall come from the rising and setting [sun] and shall lie down at table with Abraham, and Isaac, and Jacob in the kingdom of the heavens;

12 but the [false] sons of the kingdom shall be cast out into the outer darkness: there shall be the weeping and the gnashing of teeth.

13 And Yehoshua said to the centurion, Go, and as you have believed, be it to you. And his servant was healed in that hour.

Luke 7:10 And they who had been sent returning to the house found the servant, who was ill, in good health.

Widow's Son Raised from the Dead

11 And it came to pass afterwards he went into a city called Nain, and many of his disciples and a great crowd went with him.

12 And as he drew near to the gate of the city, behold, a dead man was carried out, the only son of his mother, and she a widow, and a very considerable crowd of the city [was] with her.

13 And the Lord, seeing her, was moved with compassion for her, and said to her, Weep not;

14 and coming up he touched the coffin, and the bearers stopped. And he said, Youth, I say to you, Wake up.

15 And the dead sat up and began to speak; and he gave him to his mother.

16 And fear seized on all, and they glorified the God, saying, A great prophet has been raised up among us; and the God has visited his people.

17 And this report went out in all Judea concerning him, and in all the surrounding country.

Disciples of John the Baptist Sent to Question Yehoshua If He was the One

18 And the disciples of John brought him word concerning all these things:

19 and John, having called two of his disciples, sent to Yehoshua, saying, Are you The Coming One, or are we to wait for another?

20 But the men having come to him said, John the Baptist has sent us to you, saying, Are you he The Coming One, or are we to wait for another?

21 In that hour he healed many of diseases and plagues and evil spirits, and to many blind he granted sight.

22 And Yehoshua answering said to them, Go, bring back word to John of what you have seen and heard: that blind see, lame walk, lepers are cleansed, deaf hear, dead are raised, poor are evangelized;

23 and blessed is whosoever shall not be offended in me.

Yehoshua Praises John

24 And the messengers of John having departed, he began to speak to the crowds concerning John: What went you out into the wilderness to behold? a reed shaken by the wind?

25 But what went you out to see? a man clothed in delicate garments? Behold, those who are in splendid clothing and live luxuriously are in the courts of kings.

26 But what went you out to see? a prophet? Yes, I say to you, and [what is] more excellent than a prophet.

27 This is he concerning whom it is written, Behold, I send my messenger before your face, who shall prepare your way before you;

28 for I say unto you, Among them that are born of women a greater [prophet] is no one than John [the baptist] but he who is a little one in the kingdom of the God is greater than he.

Matt 11:7 But as they went [away] Yehoshua began to say to the crowds concerning John, What went you out into the wilderness to see? a reed moved about by the wind?

8 But what went you out to see? a man clothed in delicate raiment? behold, those who wear delicate things are in the houses of kings.

9 But what went you out to see? a prophet? Yes, I say to you, and more than a prophet:

10 this is he of whom it is written, Behold, I send my messenger before your face, who shall prepare your way before you.

11 Truly I say to you, that there is not arisen among the born of women a greater than John the Baptist. But he who is a little one in the kingdom of the heavens is greater than he.

12 But from the days of John the Baptist until now, the kingdom of the heavens is taken by violence, and the violent seize on it.

13 For all the prophets and the law have prophesied unto John.

14 And if you will receive it, this is Elijah, who is to come.

15 He that has ears to hear, let him hear.

Luke 7:29 And all the people who heard [it] and the tax-gatherers, justified the God, having been baptized with the baptism of John;

30 but the Pharisees and the lawyers rendered null as to themselves the counsel of the God, not having been baptized by him.

Yehoshua Foretells Judgment

Matt 11:20 Then began he to reproach the cities in which most of his works of power had taken place, because they had not repented.

21 Woe to you, Chorazin! woe to you Beth-saida! for if the works of power which have taken place in you, had

taken place in Tyre and Sidon, they had long ago repented in sackcloth and ashes.

22 But I say to you, that it shall be more tolerable for Tyre and Sidon in judgment-day than for you.

23 And you, Capernaum, who have been raised up to heaven, shall be brought down even to hell [Hades]. For if the works of power which have taken place in you, had taken place in Sodom, it had remained until this day.

24 But I say to you, that it shall be more tolerable for the land of Sodom in judgment-day than for you.

25 At that time, Yehoshua answering said, I praise you, Father, Lord of the heaven and of the earth, that you have hid these things from the wise and prudent, and have revealed them to babes.

26 Yes, Father, for thus has it been well-pleasing in your sight.

27 All things have been delivered to me by my Father, and no one knows the Son but the Father, nor does any one know the Father, but the Son, and he to whom the Son may be pleased to reveal him.

Yehoshua Rebukes His Rejection by the People

Luke 7:31 To whom therefore shall I liken the men of this generation, and to whom are they like?

32 They are like children sitting in the market-place, and calling one to another and saying, We have piped to you, and you have not danced; we have mourned to you, and you have not wept.

33 For John the Baptist has come neither eating bread nor drinking wine, and you say, He has a daemon.

34 The Son of man has come eating and drinking, and you say, Behold an eater and wine-drinker, a friend of tax-gatherers and sinners;

35 and wisdom has been justified of all her children.

Woman Anoints Yehoshua's Feet

36 But one of the Pharisees begged him that he would eat with him. And entering into the house of the Pharisee he took his place at table;

37 and behold, a woman in the city, who was a sinner, and knew that he was sitting at meat in the house of the Pharisee, having taken an alabaster box of myrrh,

38 and standing at his feet behind him weeping, began to wash his feet with tears; and she wiped them with the hairs of her head, and kissed his feet, and anointed [them] with the myrrh.

39 And the Pharisee who had invited him, seeing it, spoke with himself saying, This [person] if he were a prophet would have known who and what the woman is who touches him, for she is a sinner.

40 And Yehoshua answering said to him, Simon, I have somewhat to say to you. And he says, Teacher, say [it]

41 There were two debtors of a certain creditor: one owed five hundred denarii and the other fifty;

42 but as they had nothing to pay, he forgave both of them [their debt] [say] which of them therefore will love him most?

43 And Simon answering said, I suppose he to whom he forgave the most. And he said to him, You have rightly judged.

44 And turning to the woman he said to Simon, See you this woman? I entered into your house; you gave me not water on my feet, but she has washed my feet with tears, and wiped them with her hair.

45 You gave me not a kiss, but she from the time I came in has not ceased kissing my feet.

46 My head with oil you did not anoint, but she has anointed my feet with myrrh.

47 For which cause I say to you, Her many sins are forgiven; for she loved much; but he to whom little is forgiven loves little.

48 And he said to her, Your sins are forgiven.

49 And they that were with [them] at table began to say within themselves, Who is this who forgives also sins?

50 And he said to the woman, Your faith has saved you; go in peace.

Yehoshua Teaches City to City; Women Support Yehoshua

Luke 8:1 And it came to pass afterwards that he went through [the country] city by city, and village by village, preaching and announcing the good news of the kingdom of the God; and the twelve [were] with him,

2 and certain women who had been healed of wicked spirits and infirmities, Mary who was called Magdalene, from whom seven daemons had gone out,

3 and Joanna, wife of Chuza, Herod's steward, and Susanna, and many others, who ministered to him of their substance.

Yehoshua Accused of being Possessed

Mark 3:20 And again a crowd comes together, so that they cannot even eat bread.

Matt 12::22 Then was brought to him one possessed by a daemon, blind and mute, and he healed him, so that the mute [man] spoke and saw.

23 And all the crowds were amazed and said, Is this [man] the Son of David?

24 But the Pharisees, having heard [it] said, This [man] does not cast out daemons, but by Beelzebub, prince of daemons.

25 But he, knowing their thoughts, said to them, Every kingdom divided against itself is brought to desolation, and every city or house divided against itself will not subsist.

26 And if Satan casts out Satan, he is divided against himself; how then shall his kingdom subsist?

27 And if I cast out daemons by Beelzebub, your sons, by whom do they cast [them] out? For this reason they shall be your judges.

28 But if I by the Spirit of God cast out daemons, then indeed the kingdom of the God is come upon you.

29 Or how can any one enter into the house of the strong [man] and plunder his goods, unless first he bind the strong [man] and then he will plunder his house.

30 He that is not with me is against me, and he that gathers not with me scatters.

Blasphemy against the Spirit

31 For this reason I say unto you, Every sin and injurious speaking shall be forgiven to men, but speaking injuriously of the Spirit shall not be forgiven to men.

32 And whosoever shall have spoken a word against the Son of man, it shall be forgiven him; but whosoever shall speak against the Holy Spirit, it shall not be forgiven him, neither in this age [aeon] nor in the coming [one]

33 Either make the tree good, and its fruit good; or make the tree corrupt, and its fruit corrupt. For from the fruit the tree is known.

34 Offspring of vipers! how can you speak good things, being wicked? For of the abundance of the heart the mouth speaks.

35 The good man out of the good treasure brings forth good things; and the wicked man out of the wicked treasure brings forth wicked things.

36 But I say unto you, that every idle word which men shall say, they shall render an account of it in judgment-day:

37 for by your words you shall be justified, and by your words you shall be condemned.

Sign of Jonah

38 Then answered him some of the scribes and Pharisees, saying, Teacher, we desire to see a sign from you.

39 But he, answering, said to them, A wicked and adulterous generation seeks after a sign, and a sign shall not be given to it except the sign of Jonas the prophet.

40 For even as Jonas was in the belly of the great fish three days and three nights, thus shall the Son of man be in the heart of the earth three days and three nights.

41 Ninevites shall stand up in the judgment with this generation, and shall condemn it: for they repented at the preaching of Jonas; and behold, more than Jonas [is] here.

42 A queen of the south shall rise up in the judgment with this generation, and shall condemn it; for she came from the ends of the earth to hear the wisdom of Solomon; and behold, more than Solomon [is] here.

Wicked Generation Cannot Clean its House of Sin

43 But when the unclean spirit has gone out of the man, he goes through dry places, seeking rest, and does not find [it]

44 Then he says, I will return to my house from where I came out; and having come, he finds [it] unoccupied, swept, and adorned.

45 Then he goes and takes with himself seven other spirits worse than himself, and entering in, they dwell there; and the last condition of that man becomes worse than the first. Thus shall it be to this wicked generation also.

[Luke 11:24 When the unclean spirit has gone out of the man, he goes through dry places seeking rest; and not finding [any] he says, I will return to my house from what place I came out.

25 And having come, he finds it swept and adorned.

26 Then he goes and takes seven other spirits worse than himself, and entering in, they dwell there; and the last condition of that man becomes worse than the first.]

Who is Yehoshua's Family?

Matt 12:46 But while he was yet speaking to the crowds, behold, his mother and his brethren stood outside, seeking to speak to him.

47 Then one said unto him, Behold, your mother and your brethren are standing outside, seeking to speak to you.

48 But he answering said to him that spoke to him, Who is my mother, and who are my brethren?

49 And, stretching out his hand to his disciples, he said, Behold my mother and my brethren;

50 for whosoever shall do the will of my Father who is in the heavens, he is my brother, and sister, and mother.

Luke 11:27 And it came to pass as he spoke these things, a certain woman, lifting up her voice out of the crowd, said to him, Blessed is the womb that has borne you, and the breasts which you have sucked.

28 But he said, Yes rather, blessed are they who hear the word of the God and keep [it]

Light and Darkness

33 But no one having lit a lamp sets it in secret, nor under the grain-measure, but on the lamp-stand, that they who enter in may see the light.

34 The lamp of the body is your eye: when your eye is whole, your whole body also is light; but when it is wicked, your body also is dark.

35 See therefore that the light which is in you be not darkness.

36 If therefore your whole body [is] light, not having any part dark, it shall be all light as when the lamp lights you with its brightness.

Hypocrisy and Pharisees

37 But as he spoke, a certain Pharisee asked him that he would dine with him; and entering in he placed himself at table.

38 But the Pharisee seeing [it] wondered that he had not first washed before dinner.

39 But the Lord said to him, Now do you Pharisees cleanse the outside of the cup and of the dish, but your inward [parts] are full of plunder and wickedness.

40 Fools, has not he who has made the outside made the inside also?

41 But rather give alms of what you have, and behold, all things are clean to you.

42 But woe unto you, Pharisees, for you pay tithes of mint and rue and every herb, and pass by the judgment and the love of the God: these you ought to have done, and not have left those aside.

43 Woe unto you, Pharisees, for you love the first seat in the synagogues and salutations in the market-places.

44 Woe unto you, for you are as the tombs which appear not, and the men walking over them do not know [it]

45 And one of the doctors of the law answering says to him, Teacher, in saying these things you insult us also.

46 And he said, To you also woe, doctors of the law, for you lay upon men burdens heavy to bear, and yourselves do not touch the burdens with one of your fingers.

47 Woe unto you, for you build the tombs of the prophets, but your fathers killed them.

48 You bear witness then, and consent to the works of your fathers; for they killed them, and you build [their tombs]

49 For this reason also the wisdom of the God has said, I will send to them prophets and apostles, and of these shall they kill and drive out by persecution,

50 that the blood of all the prophets which has been poured out from the foundation of the world may be required of this generation,

51 from the blood of Abel to the blood of Zacharias, who perished between the altar and the house; yes, I say to you, it shall be required of this generation.

52 Woe unto you, the doctors of the law, for you have taken away the key of knowledge; yourselves have not entered in, and those who were entering in you have hindered.

Pharisees Try to Trap Yehoshua

53 And as he said these things to them, the scribes and the Pharisees began to press him urgently, and to make him speak of many things;

54 watching him, [and seeking] to catch something out of his mouth, [that they might accuse him]

Yeast of the Pharisees

Luke 12:1 In those [times] the myriads of the crowd being gathered together, so that they trod one on another, he began to say to his disciples first, Beware of the leaven of the Pharisees, which is hypocrisy;

2 but there is nothing covered up which shall not be revealed, nor secret that shall not be known;

3 therefore whatever you have said in the darkness shall be heard in the light, and what you have spoken in the ear in chambers shall be proclaimed upon the housetops.

Fear Sin

4 But I say to you, my friends, Fear not those who kill the body and after this have no more that they can do.

5 But I will show you whom you shall fear: Fear him who after he has killed has authority to cast into hell [Gehenna]; yes, I say to you, Fear him.

6 Are not five sparrows sold for two assaria? and one of them is not forgotten before the God.

7 But even the hairs of your head are all numbered. Fear not therefore, you are better than many sparrows.

8 But I say to you, Whosoever shall acknowledge me before men, the Son of man will acknowledge him also before the angels of the God;

9 but he that shall have denied me before men shall be denied before the angels of the God;

10 and whoever shall say a word against the Son of man it shall be forgiven him; but to him that speaks injuriously against the Holy Spirit it shall not be forgiven.

Holy Spirit will give you the Words

11 But when they bring you before the synagogues and rulers and the authorities, be not concerned how or what you shall answer, or what you shall say;

12 for the Holy Spirit shall teach you in the hour itself what should be said.

Foolish Rich Man

13 And a person said to him out of the crowd, Teacher, speak to my brother to divide the inheritance with me.

14 But he said to him, Man, who established me [as] a judge or a divider over you?

15 And he said to them, Take heed and keep yourselves from all covetousness, for [it is] not because a man is in abundance that his life is in his possessions.

16 And he spoke a parable to them, saying, The land of a certain rich man brought forth abundantly.

17 And he reasoned within himself saying, What shall I do? for I have not [a place] where I shall lay up my fruits.

18 And he said, This will I do: I will take away my granaries and build greater, and there I will lay up all my produce and my good things;

19 and I will say to my soul, Soul, you have much good things laid by for many years; rest yourself, eat, drink, be merry.

20 But the God said to him, Fool, this night your soul shall be required of you; and who shall own what you have prepared?

Treasures on Earth not Treasures toward God

21 Thus is he who lays up treasure for himself, and is not rich toward God.

22 And he said to his disciples, For this cause I say unto you, Be not concerned for your soul, what you shall eat, nor for the body, what you shall put on.

23 The soul is more than food, and the body than raiment.

24 Consider the ravens, that they sow not nor reap; which have neither storehouse nor granary; and the God feeds them. How much better are you than the birds?

25 But which of you by being concerned can add to his stature one cubit?

26 If therefore you cannot [do] even what is least, why are you concerned about the rest?

27 Consider the lilies how they grow: they neither toil nor spin; but I say unto you, Not even Solomon in all his glory was clothed as one of these.

28 But if the God thus clothe the grass, which today is in the field and tomorrow is cast into the oven, how much rather you, O you of little faith?

29 And you, seek not what you shall eat or what you shall drink, and be not in anxiety;

30 for all these things do the nations of the world seek after, and your Father knows that you have need of these things;

31 but seek his kingdom, and [all] these things shall be added to you.

32 Fear not, little flock, for it has been the good pleasure of your Father to give you the kingdom.

33 Sell what you possess and give alms; make to yourselves purses which do not grow old, a treasure which does not fail in the heavens, where thief does not draw near nor moth destroy.

34 For where your treasure is, there also will your heart be.

Watchful Servants

35 Let your loins be girded about, and lamps burning;

36 and you like men who wait their own lord whenever he may leave the wedding, that when he comes and knocks, they may open to him immediately.

37 Blessed are those servants whom the lord [on] coming shall find watching; truly I say unto you, that he will gird himself and make them recline at table, and coming up will serve them.

38 And if he come in the second watch, and come in the third watch, and find [them] thus, blessed are those [servants]

39 But this know, that if the master of the house had known in what hour the thief was coming, he would have watched, and not have permitted his house to be dug through.

40 And you therefore, be you ready, that in the hour in which you do not think [it] the Son of man comes.

41 And Peter said to him, Lord, do you say this parable to us, or also to all?

42 And the Lord said, Who then is the faithful and prudent steward, whom his lord will set over his household, to give the measure of grain in season?

43 Blessed is that servant whom his lord [on] coming shall find doing thus;

44 truly I say unto you, that he will set him over all that he has.

45 But if that servant should say in his heart, My lord delays to come, and begin to beat the menservants and the maidservants, and to eat and to drink and to be drunken,

46 the lord of that servant shall come in a day when he does not expect it, and in an hour he knows not of, and shall cut him in two and appoint his portion with the unbelievers.

47 But that servant who knew his own lord's will, and had not prepared [himself] nor done his will, shall be beaten with many [stripes]

48 but he who knew [it] not, and did things worthy of stripes, shall be beaten with few. And to every one to whom much has been given, much shall be required from him; and to whom [men] have committed much, they will ask from him the more.

Division Predicted

49 I have come to cast a fire on the earth; and what will I if already it has been kindled?

50 But I have a baptism to be baptized with, and how am I straitened until it shall have been accomplished!

51 Think you that I have come to give peace in the earth? No, I say to you, but rather division:

52 for from henceforth there shall be five in one house divided; three shall be divided against two, and two against three:

53 father against son, and son against father; mother against daughter, and daughter against mother; a mother-in-law against her daughter-in-law, and a daughter-in-law against her mother- in-law.

Interpreting the Times

54 And he said also to the crowds, When you see a cloud rising out of the west, straightway you say, A shower is coming; and so it happens.

55 And when [you see] the south wind blow, you say, There will be heat; and it happens.

56 Hypocrites, you know how to judge of the appearance of the earth and of the heaven; how [is it then that] you do not discern this time?

57 And why among yourselves don't you judge what is right?

58 For as you go with your adverse party before a magistrate, strive in the way to be reconciled with him, lest he drag you away to the judge, and the judge shall deliver you to the officer, and the officer cast you into prison.

59 I say unto you, You shall in no way come out from there until you have paid the very last mite.

Worst Sinners Punished? Unless you Repent ...

Luke 13:1 Now at the same time there were present some who told him of the Galileans whose blood Pilate mingled with [that of] their sacrifices.

2 And he answering said to them, Think you that these Galileans were sinners beyond all the Galileans because they permitted such things?

3 No, I say to you, but if you repent not, you shall all perish in the same manner.

4 Or those eighteen on whom the tower in Siloam fell and killed them, think you that they were debtors beyond all the men who dwell in Jerusalem?

5 No, I say to you, but if you repent not, you shall all perish in like manner.

Unfruitful Fig Tree

6 And he spoke this parable: A certain [man] had a fig-tree planted in his vineyard, and he came seeking fruit upon it and did not find [any]

7 And he said to the vinedresser, Behold, [these] three years I come seeking fruit on this fig-tree and find none: cut it down; why does it also render the ground useless?

8 But he answering says to him, Sir, leave it alone for this year also, until I shall dig about it and put dung,

9 and if it shall bear fruit – but if not, after that you shall cut it down.

Healing on the Sabbath

10 And he was teaching in one of the synagogues on the sabbaths.

11 And lo, [there was] a woman having a spirit of infirmity eighteen years, and she was bent together and wholly unable to lift her head up.

12 And Yehoshua, seeing her, called to [her] and said to her, Woman, you are loosed from your infirmity.

13 And he laid his hands upon her; and immediately she was made straight, and glorified the God.

14 But the ruler of the synagogue, indignant because Yehoshua healed on the Sabbath, answering said to the crowd, There are six days in which [people] ought to work; in these

therefore come and be healed, and not on the Sabbath day.

15 The Lord therefore answered him and said, Hypocrites! does not each one of you on the Sabbath loose his ox or his donkey from the manger and leading [it] away, water [it]

16 And this [woman] who is a daughter of Abraham, whom Satan has bound, lo, [these] eighteen years, ought she not to be loosed from this bond on the Sabbath day?

17 And as he said these things, all who were opposed to him were ashamed; and all the crowd rejoiced at all the glorious things which were being done by him.

Parable of the Sower

Matt 13:1 And that [same] day Yehoshua went out from the house and sat down by the sea.

2 And great crowds were gathered together to him, so that going on board ship himself he sat down, and the whole crowd stood on the shore.

3 And he spoke to them many things in parables, saying, Behold, the sower went out to sow:

4 and as he sowed, some [grains] fell along the way, and the birds came and devoured them;

5 and others fell upon the rocky places where they had not much earth, and immediately they sprang up out of [the ground] because of not having [any] depth of earth,

6 but when the sun rose they were burned up, and because of not having [any] root were dried up;

7 and others fell upon the thorns, and the thorns grew up and choked them;

8 and others fell upon the good ground, and produced fruit, one a hundred, one sixty, and one thirty.

9 He that has ears, let him hear.

Purpose of Parables: To Hide

10 And the disciples came up and said to him, Why do you speak to them in parables?

11 And he answering said to them, Because to you it is given to know the mysteries of the kingdom of the heavens, but to them it is not given;

12 for whoever has, to him shall be given, and he shall be caused to be in abundance; but he who has not, even what he has shall be taken away from him.

13 For this cause I speak to them in parables, because seeing they do not see, and hearing they do not hear nor understand;

14 and in them is fulfilled the prophecy of Isaiah, which says, Hearing you shall hear and shall not understand, and beholding you shall behold and not see;

15 for the heart of this people has grown fat, and they have heard heavily with their ears, and they have closed their eyes as asleep, lest they should see with the eyes, and hear with the ears, and understand with the heart, and should be converted, and I should heal them.

16 But blessed are your eyes because they see, and your ears because they hear;

17 for truly I say unto you, that many prophets and righteous [men] have desired to see the things which you behold and did not see [them] and to hear the things which you hear and did not hear [them]

Meaning of the Sower Parable

18 You, therefore, hear the parable of the sower.

19 From every one who hears the word of the kingdom and does not understand [it] the wicked one comes and catches away what was sown in his heart: this is he that is sown by the wayside.

20 But he that is sown on the rocky places – this is he who hears the word and immediately receives it with joy,

21 but has no root in himself, but is for a time only; and when tribulation or persecution happens on account of the word, he is immediately offended.

22 And he that is sown among the thorns – this is he who hears the word, and the concerns of this life, and the deceit of riches choke the word, and he becomes unfruitful.

23 But he that is sown upon the good ground – this is he who hears and understands the word, who bears fruit also, and produces, one a hundred, one sixty, and one thirty.

Parable of Weeds

24 Another parable set he before them, saying, The kingdom of the heavens has become like a man sowing good seed in his field;

25 but while men slept, his enemy came and sowed weeds among the wheat, and went away.

26 But when the blade shot up and produced fruit, then appeared the weeds also.

27 And the servants of the householder came up and said to him, Sir, have you not sown good seed in your field? From where came the weeds?

28 And he said to them, A man [that is] an enemy has done this. And the servants said to him, Will you then that we should go and gather it [up]

29 But he said, No; lest [in] gathering the weeds you should root up the wheat with it.

30 Permit both to grow together unto the harvest, and in time of the harvest I will say to the harvestmen, Gather first the weeds, and bind them into bundles to burn; but the wheat bring together into my granary.

31 Another parable set he before them, saying, The kingdom of the heavens is like a grain of mustard [seed] which a man took and sowed in his field;

32 which is less indeed than all seeds, but when it is grown is greater than herbs, and becomes a tree, so that the birds of heaven come and roost in its branches.

33 He spoke another parable to them: The kingdom of the heavens is like leaven, which a woman took and hid in three measures of meal until it had been all leavened.

Yehoshua only Spoke in Parables

34 All these things Yehoshua spoke to the crowds in parables, and outside a parable he did not speak to them,

35 so that that should be fulfilled which was spoken through the prophet, saying, I will open my mouth in parables; I will utter things hidden from the world's foundation.

Parable of Weeds Explained

36 Then, having dismissed the crowds, he went into the house; and his disciples came to him, saying, Expound to us the parable of the weeds of the field.

37 But he answering said, He that sows the good seed is the Son of man,

38 and the field is the world; and the good seed, these are the sons of the kingdom, but the weeds are the sons of the evil [one]

39 and the enemy who has sowed it is the evil mind [daemon other mind; devil] and the harvest is the completion of the age [aeon] and the harvest men are angels.

40 As then the weeds are gathered and burned in the fire, thus it shall be in the completion of the age [aeon]

41 The Son of man shall send his angels, and they shall gather out of his kingdom all offences, and those that practice lawlessness;

42 and they shall cast them into the furnace of fire; there shall be the weeping and the gnashing of teeth.

43 Then the righteous shall shine forth as the sun in the kingdom of their Father. He that has ears, let him hear.

Parable of the Lamp

Mark 4:21 And he said to them, Does the lamp come that it should be put under the bushel or under the couch? [is it] not that it should be set upon the lamp-stand?

22 For there is nothing hidden which shall not be made manifest; nor does any secret thing take place, but that it should come to light.

23 If any one have ears to hear, let him hear.

24 And he said to them, Take heed what you hear; with what measure you measured, it shall be measured to you; and there shall be [more] added to you.

25 For whosoever has, to him shall be given; and he who has not, even what he has shall be taken from him.

Parable of the Seed

26 And he said, Thus is the kingdom of the God, as if a man should cast the seed upon the earth,

27 and should sleep and rise up night and day, and the seed should sprout and grow, he does not know how.

28 The earth bears fruit of itself, first the blade, then an ear, then full grain in the ear.

29 But when the fruit is produced, immediately he sends the sickle, for the harvest is come.

Parable of Hidden Treasure

Matt 13:44 The kingdom of the heavens is like a treasure hid in the field, which a man having found has hid, and for the joy of it goes and sells all whatever he has, and buys that field.

Parable of the Pearl

45 Again, the kingdom of the heavens is like a merchant seeking beautiful pearls;

46 and having found one pearl of great value, he went and sold all whatever he had and bought it.

Parable of the Net

47 Again, the kingdom of the heavens is like a net which has been cast into the sea, and which has gathered together of every kind,

48 which, when it has been filled, having drawn up on the shore and sat down, they gathered the good into vessels and cast the worthless out.

49 Thus shall it be in the completion of the age [aeon] the angels shall go forth and sever the wicked from the midst of the just,

50 and shall cast them into the furnace of fire; there shall be the weeping and the gnashing of teeth.

Parable of New and Old Treasure

51 Yehoshua says to them, Have you understood all these things? They say to him, Yes, [lord]

52 And he said to them, For this reason every scribe discipled to the kingdom of the heavens is like a man [that is] a householder who brings out of his treasure things new and old.

Mark 4 33 And with many such parables he spoke the word to them, as they were able to hear,

Matt 13:34 but without a parable spoke he not to them; and in private he explained all things to his disciples.

34 All these things Yehoshua spoke to the crowds in parables, and outside a parable he did not speak to them,

35 so that that should be fulfilled which was spoken through the prophet, saying, I will open my mouth in parables; I will utter things hidden from the world's foundation.

Matt 13:53 And it came to pass when Yehoshua had finished these parables he withdrew from there.

Followers of Yehoshua Challenged

Matt 8:18 And Yehoshua, seeing great crowds around him, commanded to depart to the other side.

19 And a scribe came up and said to him, Teacher, I will follow you wherever you may go.

20 And Yehoshua says to him, The foxes have holes, and the birds of the heaven nests; but the Son of man has nowhere he may lay his head.

21 But another of his disciples said to him, Lord, permit me first to go away and bury my father.

22 But Yehoshua said to him, Follow me, and leave the dead to bury their own dead.

> Luke 9:57 And it came to pass as they went in the way, one said to him, I will follow you wheresoever you go, Lord.
>
> 58 And Yehoshua said to him, The foxes have holes and the birds of the heaven nests, but the Son of man has not where he may lay his head.
>
> 59 And he said to another, Follow me. But he said, Lord, allow me to go first and bury my father.
>
> 60 But Yehoshua said to him, Permit the dead to bury their own dead, but do you go and announce the kingdom of the God.
>
> 61 And another also said, I will follow you, Lord, but first allow me to bid good-by to those at my house.
>
> 62 But Yehoshua said to him, No one having laid his hand on the plough and looking back is fit for the kingdom of the God.

Yehoshua Calms the Sea

Mark 4:35 And on that day, when evening was come, he says to them, Let us go over to the other side:

36 and having sent away the crowd, they take him with [them] as he was, in the ship. But other ships also were with him.

37 And there comes a violent gust of wind, and the waves beat into the ship, so that it already filled.

38 And he was in the stern sleeping on the cushion. And they awake him up and say to him, Teacher, do you not care that we are perishing?

39 And awaking up he rebuked the wind, and said to the sea, Silence; be mute. And the wind fell, and there was a great calm.

40 And he said to them, Why are you [thus] fearful? how [is it] you have not faith?

41 And they feared [with] great fear, and said one to another, Who then is this, that even the wind and the sea obey him?

Demon-Possessed Cured in the Gerasene Region

Mark 5:1 And they came to the other side of the sea, to the country of the Gadarenes.

2 And immediately on his going out of the ship there met him out of the tombs a man possessed by an unclean spirit,

3 who had his dwelling in the tombs; and no one was able to bind him, not even with chains;

4 because he had been often bound with fetters and chains, and the chains had been torn asunder by him, and the fetters were shattered; and no one was able to subdue him.

5 And continually night and day, in the tombs and in the mountains, he was crying and cutting himself with stones.

6 But seeing Yehoshua from afar off, he ran and did him homage,

7 and crying with a loud voice he says, What have I to do with you, Yehoshua, Son of the Most High God? I adjure you by the God, torment me not.

8 For he said to him, Come forth, unclean spirit, out of the man.

9 And he asked him, What is your name? And he says to him, Legion is my name, because we are many.

10 And he besought him much that he would not send them away out of the country.

11 Now there was there just at the mountain a great herd of swine feeding;

12 and they besought him, saying, Send us into the swine that we may enter into them.

13 And Yehoshua [immediately] allowed them. And the unclean spirits going out entered into the swine, and the herd rushed down the steep slope, into the sea about two thousand, and were choked in the sea.

14 And those that were feeding them fled and reported it in the city and in the country. And they went out to see what it was that had taken place.

15 And they come to Yehoshua, and they see the possessed of daemons sitting [and] clothed and sensible, him that had had the legion: and they were afraid.

16 And they that had seen [it] related to them how it had happened to the [man] possessed by daemons, and concerning the swine.

17 And they began to beg him to depart from their coasts.

18 And as he went on board ship, the man that had been possessed by daemons besought him that he might be with him.

19 And he permitted him not, but says to him, Go to your home to your own people, and tell them how great things the Lord has done for you, and has had mercy on you.

20 And he went away and began to proclaim in the Decapolis how great things Yehoshua had done for him; and all wondered.

Jairus, Ruler of the Snyagogue, Asks Yehoshua to Heal his Daughter

21 And Yehoshua having passed over in the ship again to the other side, a great crowd gathered to him; and he was by the sea.

22 And [behold] there comes one of the rulers of the synagogue, by name Jairus, and seeing him, falls down at his feet;

23 and he besought him much, saying, My little daughter is at extremity; [I pray] that you should come and lay your hands upon her so that she may be healed, and may live.

24 And he went with him, and a large crowd followed him and pressed on him.

Woman Healed by Touching Yehoshua's Apparel

25 And a certain woman who had had a flux of blood twelve years,

26 and had suffered much under many physicians, and had spent everything she had and had found no advantage from it, but had rather got worse,

27 having heard concerning Yehoshua, came in the crowd behind and touched his clothes;

28 for she said, If I shall touch but his clothes I shall be healed.

29 And immediately her fountain of blood was dried up, and she knew in her body that she was cured from the scourge.

30 And immediately Yehoshua, knowing in himself the power that had gone out

of him, turning round in the crowd said, Who has touched my clothes?

31 And his disciples said to him, You see the crowd pressing on you, and you said, Who touched me?

32 And he looked round about to see her who had done this.

33 But the woman, frightened and trembling, knowing what had taken place in her, came and fell down before him, and told him all the truth.

34 And he said to her, Daughter, your faith has healed you; go in peace, and be well of your scourge.

Jairus' Daughter Raised from the Dead

35 While he was yet speaking, they come from the ruler of the synagogue's [house] saying, Your daughter has died, why trouble you the teacher any further?

36 But Yehoshua [immediately] having heard the word spoken, says to the ruler of the synagogue, Fear not; only believe.

37 And he permitted no one to accompany him except Peter and James, and John the brother of James.

38 And he comes to the house of the ruler of the synagogue, and sees the tumult, and people weeping and wailing greatly.

39 And entering in he says to them, Why do you make a tumult and weep? the child has not died, but sleeps.

40 And they derided him. But he, having put [them] all out, takes with him the father of the child, and the mother, and those that were with him, and enters in where the child was lying.

41 And having laid hold of the hand of the child, he says to her, Talitha koumi, which is, interpreted, Damsel, I say to you, Arise.

42 And immediately the damsel arose and walked, for she was of years twelve.

And they were astonished with great astonishment.

43 And he charged them much that no one should know this; and he desired that [something] should be given her to eat.

Two Blind Healed

Matt 9:27 And as Yehoshua passed on from there, two blind [men] followed him, crying and saying, Have mercy on us, Son of David.

28 And when he was come to the house, the blind [men] came to him. And Yehoshua says to them, Do you believe that I am able to do this? They say to him, Yes, Lord.

29 Then he touched their eyes, saying, According to your faith, be it unto you.

30 And their eyes were opened; and Yehoshua charged them sharply, saying, See, let no man know it.

31 But they, when they were gone out, spread his name abroad in all that land.

Mute Healed

32 But as these were going out, behold, they brought to him a mute man possessed by a daemon.

33 And the daemon having been cast out, the mute spoke. And the crowds were astonished, saying, It has never been seen thus in Israel.

34 But the Pharisees said, He casts out the daemons through the prince of the daemons.

Yehoshua Rejected again in his Hometown

Mark 6:1 And he went out from there and came to his own country, and his disciples follow him.

2 And when Sabbath was come he began to teach in the synagogue, and many hearing were amazed, saying, From where [has] this [man] these things? and what [is] the wisdom that is

given to him, and such works of power are done by his hands?

3 Is not this the carpenter, the son of Mary, and brother of James, and Joses, and Judas, and Simon? and are not his sisters here with us? And they were offended in him.

4 But Yehoshua said to them, A prophet is not despised except in his own country, and among [his] kinsmen, and in his own house.

5 And he could not do any work of power there, except that laying his hands on a few infirm persons he healed [them]

6 And he wondered because of their unbelief. And he went round the villages in a circuit, teaching.

Need for Workers

Matt 9: 35 And Yehoshua went round all the cities and the villages, teaching in their synagogues, and preaching the good news of the kingdom, and healing every disease and every bodily weakness.

36 But when he saw the crowds he was moved with compassion for them, because they were harassed, and cast away as sheep not having a shepherd.

37 Then says he to his disciples, The harvest [is] great and the workmen [are] few;

38 supplicate therefore the Lord of the harvest, that he send forth workmen unto his harvest.

Apostles Given Power and Instructions

Matt 10:1 And having called to him his twelve disciples, he gave them power over unclean spirits, so that they should cast them out, and heal every disease and every bodily weakness.

2 Now the names of the twelve apostles are these: first, Simon, who was called Peter, and Andrew his brother; James

the [son] of Zebedee, and John his brother;

3 Philip and Bartholomew; Thomas, and Matthew the tax-gatherer; James the [son] of Alphaeus, and Lebbaeus, who was surnamed Thaddaeus;

4 Simon the Cananaean, and Judas the Iscariote, who also delivered him up.

5 These twelve Yehoshua sent out when he had charged them, saying, Go not off into the way of the nations, and into a city of Samaritans enter you not;

6 but go rather to the lost sheep of the house of Israel.

7 And as you go, preach, saying, The kingdom of the heavens has drawn near.

8 Heal the infirm, [raise the dead] cleanse lepers, cast out daemons: you have received freely, give freely.

9 Do not provide yourselves with gold, or silver, or brass, for your belts,

10 nor scrip for the way, nor two body coats, nor sandals, nor a staff: for the workman is worthy of his nourishment.

Stay Only Where You Are Wanted

11 But into whatsoever city or village you enter, inquire who in it is worthy, and there remain till you go forth.

12 And as you enter into a house salute it.

13 And if the house indeed be worthy, let your peace come upon it; but if it be not worthy, let your peace return to you.

Depart From Where You Are Not Wanted

14 And whosoever shall not receive you, nor hear your words, as you go forth out of that house or city, shake off the dust of your feet.

15 Truly I say unto you, It shall be more tolerable for the land of Sodom and Gomorrha in judgment-day than for that city.

Sheep in the Midst of Wolves

16 Behold, I send you as sheep in the midst of wolves; be therefore prudent as the serpents, and guileless as the doves.

17 But beware of men; for they will deliver you up to sanhedrims, and scourge you in their synagogues;

18 and you shall be brought before rulers and kings for my sake, for a testimony to them and to the nations.

19 But when they deliver you up, be not concerned how or what you shall speak; for it shall be given to you in that hour what you shall speak.

20 For you are not the speakers, but the Spirit of your Father which speaks in you.

21 But brother shall deliver up brother to death, and father child; and children shall rise up against parents and shall put them to death;

22 and you shall be hated of all on account of my name. But he that has endured to the end, he shall be saved.

23 But when they persecute you in this city, flee to the other; for truly I say to you, You shall not have completed the cities of Israel until the Son of man be come.

24 The disciple is not above his teacher, nor the servant above his lord.

25 [It is] sufficient for the disciple that he should become as his teacher, and the servant as his lord. If they have called the master of the house Beelzebub, how much more those of his household?

26 Fear them not therefore; for there is nothing covered which shall not be revealed, and secret which shall not be known.

27 What I say to you in darkness speak in the light, and what you hear in the ear preach upon the houses.

28 And be not afraid of those who kill the body, but cannot kill the soul; but fear rather him who is able to destroy both soul and body in hell [Gehenna].

29 Are not two sparrows sold for a quarter [quadrans] and one of them shall not fall to the ground without [knowing] your Father;

30 but of you even the hairs of the head are all numbered.

31 Fear not therefore; you are better than many sparrows.

32 Every one therefore who shall acknowledge me before men, I also will acknowledge him before my Father who is in the heavens.

33 But whosoever shall deny me before men, him will I also deny before my Father who is in the heavens.

34 Do not think that I have come to send peace upon the earth: I have not come to send peace, but a sword.

35 For I have come to set a man at variance with his father, and the daughter with her mother, and the daughter-in-law with her mother-in-law;

36 and they of his household [shall be] a man's enemies.

37 He who loves father or mother above me is not worthy of me; and he who loves son or daughter above me is not worthy of me.

38 And he who does not take up his cross and follow after me is not worthy of me.

39 He that finds his soul shall lose it, and he who has lost his soul for my sake shall find it.

40 He that receives you receives me, and he that receives me receives him that sent me.

41 He that receives a prophet in the name of a prophet, shall receive a prophet's reward; and he that receives a righteous man in the name of a

righteous man, shall receive a righteous man's reward.

42 And whosoever shall give to drink to one of these little ones a cup of cold [water] only, in the name of a disciple, truly I say unto you, he shall in no way lose his reward.

Teaching Village to Village

Matt 11:1 And it came to pass when Yehoshua had finished commanding his twelve disciples, he departed from there to teach and preach in their cities.

Luke 9:6 And going forth they passed through the villages, announcing the good news and healing everywhere.

Herod Hears of Yehoshua

Mark 6:14 And Herod the king heard [of him] for his name had become public, and said, John the Baptist is risen from among the dead, and on this account works of power are worked by him.

15 And others said, It is Elijah; and others said, It is a prophet, as one of the prophets.

16 But Herod when he heard [it] said, John whom I beheaded, he it is; he is risen [from among the dead]

Luke 9:7 And Herod the tetrarch heard of all the things which were done [by him] and was in perplexity, because it was said by some that John was risen from among the dead,

8 and by some that Elijah had appeared, and by others that one of the old prophets had risen again.

9 And Herod said, John I have beheaded, but who is this of whom I hear such things? and he sought to see him.

Death of John the Baptist

Mark 6:17 For the same Herod had sent and seized John, and had bound him in prison on account of Herodias, the wife of Philip his brother, because he had married her.

18 For John said to Herod, It is not lawful for you to have the wife of your brother.

19 But Herodias kept it [in her mind] against him, and wished to kill him, and could not:

20 for Herod feared John knowing that he was a just and holy man, and kept him safe; and having heard him, did many things, and heard him gladly.

21 And a holiday being come, when Herod, on his birthday, made a supper to his grandees, and to the commanders, and the chief [men] of Galilee;

22 and the daughter of the same Herodias having come in, and danced, pleased Herod and those that were with him at table; and the king said to the damsel, Ask of me whatsoever you will and I will give it you.

23 And he swore to her, Whatsoever you shall ask me I will give you, to half of my kingdom.

24 And she went out, and said to her mother, What should I ask? And she said, The head of John the Baptist.

25 And immediately going in with haste to the king, she asked saying, I desire that you give me directly upon a dish the head of John the Baptist.

26 And the king, [while] made very sorry, on account of the oaths and those lying at table with him would not break his word with her.

27 And immediately the king, having sent one of the guard, ordered his head to be brought. And he went out and beheaded him in the prison,

28 and brought his head upon a dish, and gave it to the damsel, and the damsel gave it to her mother.

29 And his disciples having heard [it] came and took up his body, and laid it in a tomb.

Apostles Report Back to Yehoshua

30 And the apostles are gathered together to Yehoshua. And they related to him all things, [both] what they had done and what they had taught.

31 And he said to them, Come you yourselves alone into a desolate place and rest a little. For those coming and those going were many, and they had not leisure even to eat.

32 And they went away apart into a desolate place by ship.

33 And many saw them going, and recognized them, and ran together there on foot, out of all the cities, and got [there] before them.

Third Passover of Yehoshua's Ministry

Last Year of Ministry Begins

Yehoshua Teaches Multitude

34 And on leaving [the ship] [Yehoshua] saw a great crowd, and he was moved with compassion for them, because they were as sheep not having a shepherd. And he began to teach them many things.

Luke 9:11 But the crowds knowing [it] followed him; and he received them and spoke to them of the kingdom of the God, and cured those that had need of healing.

John 6:4 but the Passover,[16] the feast of the Jews, was near.

> [5 Yehoshua then, lifting up his eyes and seeing that a great crowd is coming to him, says to Philip, From where shall we buy loaves that these may eat?]

Yehoshua Feeds Five Thousand

Mark 6:35 And when it was already late in the day, his disciples coming to him say, The place is desolate, and it is already late in the day;

36 send them away that they may go into the country and villages around, and buy themselves bread, for they have not anything they can eat.

37 And he answering said to them, Give you them to eat. And they say to him, Shall we go and buy two hundred denarii worth of bread and give them to eat?

38 And he says to them, How many loaves have you? Go [and] see. And when they knew they say, Five, and two fishes.

39 And he ordered them to make them all sit down by companies on the green grass.

40 And they sat down in ranks by hundreds and by fifties.

41 And having taken the five loaves and the two fishes, looking up to heaven, he blessed, and broke the loaves, and gave [them] to his disciples that they might set [them] before them. And the two fishes he divided among all.

42 And they all ate and were satisfied.

43 And they took up of fragments the fillings of twelve hand- baskets, and of the fishes.

44 And those that ate of the loaves were five thousand men.

John 6:13 They gathered [them] therefore together, and filled twelve hand-baskets full of fragments of the five barley loaves, which were over and above to those that had eaten.

14 The men therefore, having seen the sign which Yehoshua had done, said, This is truly the prophet which is coming into the world.

Yehoshua Avoids Being Made King

Luke 6:45 And immediately he compelled his disciples to go on board ship, and to go on before to the other side to Beth-saida, while he sends the crowd away.

John 6:15 Yehoshua therefore knowing that they were going to come and seize him, that they might make him king, departed again to the mountain himself alone.

Yehoshua Walks on Water

16 But when evening was come, his disciples went down to the sea,

17 and having gone on board ship, they went over the sea to Capernaum. And it

---

16 3rd Passover of Ministry (2 ½ years completed with 1 year left)

had already become dark, and Yehoshua had not come to them,

18 and the sea was agitated by a strong wind blowing.

19 Having rowed then about twenty-five or thirty stadia, they see Yehoshua walking on the sea and coming near the ship; and they were frightened.

[Luke 6:46 And, having dismissed them, he departed into the mountain to pray.

47 And when evening was come, the ship was in the midst of the sea, and he alone upon the land.

48 And seeing them laboring in rowing, for the wind was contrary to them, about the fourth watch of the night he comes to them walking on the sea, and would have passed them by. 49 But they, seeing him walking on the sea, thought that it was a ghost, and cried out.]

Matt 14:26 And the disciples, seeing him walking on the sea, were troubled, saying, It is a ghost. And they cried out through fear.

27 But Yehoshua immediately spoke to them, saying, Take courage; it is I: be not afraid.

28 And Peter answering him said, Lord, if it be you, command me to come to you upon the waters.

Peter Walks on Water Also

29 And he said, Come. And Peter, having descended from the ship, walked upon the waters to go to Yehoshua.

30 But seeing the wind strong he was afraid; and beginning to sink he cried out, saying, Lord, save me.

31 And immediately Yehoshua stretched out his hand and caught hold of him, and says to him, O you of little faith, why did you doubt?

32 And when they had gone up into the ship, the wind fell.

33 But those in the ship came and did homage to him, saying, Truly you are God's Son.

Mark 6:51 And he went up to them into the ship, and the wind fell. And they were exceedingly beyond measure astonished in themselves and wondered;

52 for they understood not through the bread: for their heart was hardened.

Miracles at Gennesaret

53 And having passed over, they came to the land of Gennesaret and made the shore.

54 And on their coming out of the ship, immediately recognizing him,

55 they ran through that whole country around, and began to carry about those that were ill on couches, where they heard that he was.

56 And wherever he entered into villages, or cities, or the country, they laid the sick in the market-places, and besought him that they might touch if it were only the hem of his garment; and as many as touched him were healed.

Crowd Wonders How Yehoshua Left (not knowing he walked on water)

John 6:22 On the next day the crowd which stood on the other side of the sea, having seen that there was no other little ship there except that into which his disciples had got, and that Yehoshua had not gone with his disciples into the ship, but that his disciples had gone away alone;

23 but other little ships out of Tiberias came near to the place where they ate bread after the Lord had given thanks;

24 when therefore the crowd saw that Yehoshua was not there, nor his

disciples, they got into the ships, and came to Capernaum, seeking Yehoshua.

Bread of Life

25 And having found him the other side of the sea, they said to him, Rabbi, when did you arrive here?

26 Yehoshua answered them and said, Truly, truly, I say to you, You seek me not because you have seen signs, but because you have eaten of the loaves and been filled.

27 Work not [for] the food which perishes, but [for] the food which abides unto aeonian life, which the Son of man shall give to you; for him has the Father sealed the God.

28 They said therefore to him, What should we do that we may work the works of the God?

29 Yehoshua answered and said to them, This is the work of the God, that you believe on him whom he has sent.

30 They said therefore to him, What sign then will you do that we may see and believe you? what do you work?

31 Our fathers ate the manna in the wilderness, as it is written, He gave them bread out of heaven to eat.

32 Yehoshua therefore said to them, Truly, truly, I say to you, [it is] not Moses that has given you the bread out of heaven; but my Father gives you the true bread out of heaven.

33 For the bread of the God is he who comes down out of heaven and gives life to the world.

34 They said therefore to him, Lord, always give to us this bread.

35 [And] Yehoshua said to them, I am the bread of life: he that comes to me shall never hunger, and he that believes on me shall never thirst at any time.

36 But I have said to you, that you have also seen me and do not believe.

37 All that the Father gives me shall come to me, and him that comes to me I will not at all cast out.

38 For I am come down from heaven, not that I should do my will, but the will of him that has sent me.

39 And this is the will of him that has sent me, that of all that he has given me I should lose nothing, but should raise it up in the last day.

40 For this is the will of my Father, that every one who sees the Son, and believes on him, should have aeonian life; and I will raise him up at the last day.

41 The Jews therefore murmured about him, because he said, I am the bread which has come down out of heaven.

42 And they said, Is not this Yehoshua the son of Joseph, whose father and mother we have known? how then does he say, I am come down out of heaven?

43 Yehoshua therefore answered and said to them, Murmur not among yourselves.

44 No one can come to me except the Father who has sent me draw him, and I will raise him up in the last day.

45 It is written in the prophets, And they shall be all taught of the God. Every one that has heard from the Father and has learned, comes to me;

46 not that any one has seen the Father, except he who is of the God, he has seen the Father.

47 Truly, truly, I say to you, He that believes [on me] has aeonian life.

48 I am the bread of life.

49 Your fathers ate the manna in the wilderness and died.

50 This is the bread which comes down out of heaven, that one may eat of it and not die.

51 I am the living bread which has come down out of heaven: if any one shall

have eaten of this bread he shall live into the aeon; but the bread which I shall give is my flesh, which I will give for the life of the world.

Eating Flesh?

52 The Jews therefore contended among themselves, saying, How can he give us this flesh to eat?

53 Yehoshua therefore said to them, Truly, truly, I say unto you, Unless you shall have eaten the flesh of the Son of man, and drunk his blood, you have no life in yourselves.

54 He that eats my flesh and drinks my blood has aeonian life, and I will raise him up at the last day:

55 for my flesh is truly food and my blood is truly drink.

56 He that eats my flesh and drinks my blood dwells in me and I in him.

57 As the living Father has sent me and I live on account of the Father, he also who eats me shall live also on account of me.

58 This is the bread which has come down out of heaven. Not as the fathers ate and died: he that eats this bread shall live into the aeon.

59 These things he said in the synagogue, teaching in Capernaum.

Offended Disciples Turn Away From Yehoshua

60 Many therefore of his disciples having heard [it] said, This word is hard; who can hear it?

61 But Yehoshua, knowing in himself that his disciples murmur concerning this, said to them, Does this offend you?

62 If then you see the Son of man ascending up where he was the first?

Real Meaning of Words is Spiritual

63 It is the Spirit which gives life, the flesh profits nothing: the words which I have spoken unto you are spirit and are life.

64 But there are some of you who do not believe. For Yehoshua knew from the beginning who they were who did not believe, and who would deliver him up.

65 And he said, Therefore said I unto you, that no one can come to me unless it be given to him from the Father.

66 From that [time] many of his disciples went backwards and walked no more with him.

Peter Reaffirms Faith

67 Yehoshua therefore said to the twelve, Will you also go away?

68 Simon Peter answered him, Lord, to whom shall we go? you have words of aeonian life;

69 and we have believed and known that you are the holy one of the God.

70 Yehoshua answered them, Have not I chosen you the twelve? and of you one is a daemon.

71 Now he spoke of Judas [the son] of Simon, Iscariote, for he [it was who] should deliver him up, being one of the twelve.

Traditions of Pharisees Not God's Law

Mark 7:1 And the Pharisees and some of the scribes, coming from Jerusalem, are gathered together to him,

2 and seeing some of his disciples eat bread with defiled, that is, unwashed, hands,

3 for the Pharisees and all the Jews, unless they wash their hands diligently, do not eat, holding what has been delivered by the ancients;

4 and [on coming] from the market-place, unless they are washed, they do not eat; and there are many other things which they have received to hold, the washing of cups and vessels, and brazen utensils, and couches,

5 then the Pharisees and the scribes ask him, Why do your disciples not walk according to what has been delivered by the ancients, but eat the bread with defiled hands?

6 But he answering said to them, Well did Isaiah prophesy concerning you hypocrites, as it is written, This people honor me with their lips, but their heart is far away from me.

7 But in vain do they worship me, teaching [as their] teachings commandments of men.

8 [For,] leaving the commandment of the God, you hold what is delivered by men [to keep] – washing of vessels and cups, and many other such like things you do.

9 And he said to them, Well do you set aside the commandment of the God, that you may observe what is delivered by yourselves [to keep]

10 For Moses said, honor your father and your mother; and, he who speaks ill of father or mother, let him surely die.

11 But you say, If a man say to his father or his mother, [it is] corban that is, gift, whatsoever you might have profit from me by ...

12 And you no longer permit him to do anything for his father or his mother;

13 making void the word of the God by your traditional teaching which you have delivered; and many such like things you do.

Real Sin comes from Within

14 And having called again the crowd, he said to them, Hear me, all [of you] and understand:

15 There is nothing from outside a man entering into him which can defile him; but the things which go out from him, those it is which defile the man.

16 If any one have ears to hear, let him hear.

17 And when he went indoors from the crowd, his disciples asked him concerning the parable.

18 And he says to them, Are you also thus unintelligent? Do you not perceive that all that is outside entering into the man cannot defile him,

19 because it does not enter into his heart but into his belly, and goes out into the sewer, purging all meats?

20 And he said, That which goes forth out of the man, that defiles the man.

21 For from within, out of the heart of men, go forth evil thoughts, adulteries, fornications, murders,

22 thefts, covetousness, wickedness, deceit, licentiousness, a wicked eye, injurious language, haughtiness, folly;

23 all these wicked things go forth from within and defile the man.

Yehoshua Stayed around Galilee because the Jews wanted to Kill Him

John 7:1 And after these things Yehoshua walked in Galilee, for he would not walk in Judea, because the Jews sought to kill him.

Yehoshua's Tour throughout the Region of Galilee

Matt 15:21 And Yehoshua, going forth from there, went away into the parts of Tyre and Sidon;

Mark 7:24b and having entered into a house he would not have any one know [it] and he could not be hid.

Matt 15:22 and lo, a Canaanitish woman, coming out from those borders, cried [to him] saying, Have pity on me, Lord, Son of David; my daughter is miserably possessed by a daemon.

23 But he did not answer her a word. And his disciples came to him and asked him, saying, Dismiss her, for she cries after us.

24 But he answering said, I have not been sent except to the lost sheep of Israel's house.

25 But she came and did him homage, saying, Lord, help me.

26 But he answering said, It is not well to take the bread of the children and cast it to the dogs.

27 But she said, Yes, Lord; for even the dogs eat of the crumbs which fall from the table of their masters.

28 Then Yehoshua answering said to her, O woman, your faith [is] great. Be it to you as you desire. And her daughter was healed from that hour.

29 And Yehoshua, going away from there [vicinity of Tyre and went through Sidon - Mark 7:31], came towards the sea of Galilee, and he went up into the mountain and sat down there;

30 and great crowds came to him, having with them lame, blind, mute, crippled, and many others, and they cast them at his feet, and he healed them:

31 so that the crowds wondered, seeing mute speaking, crippled sound, lame walking, and blind seeing; and they glorified the God of Israel.

Yehoshua Feeds Four Thousand

32 But Yehoshua, having called his disciples to him said, I have compassion on the crowd, because they have stayed with me already three days and they have not anything they can eat, and I would not send them away fasting lest they should faint on the way.

33 And his disciples say to him, From where should we have so many loaves in the wilderness as to satisfy so great a crowd?

34 And Yehoshua says to them, How many loaves have you? But they said, Seven, and a few small fishes.

35 And he commanded the crowds to lie down on the ground;

36 and having taken the seven loaves and the fishes, having given thanks, he broke [them] and gave [them] to his disciples, and the disciples to the crowd.

37 And all ate and were filled; and they took up what was over and above of the fragments seven baskets full;

38 but they that ate were four thousand men, besides women and children.

39 And, having dismissed the crowds, he went on board ship and came to the borders of Magadan.

Pharisees and Sadducees ask for Sign

Matt 16:1 And the Pharisees and Sadducees, coming to him asked him, tempting him to show them a sign out of heaven.

2 But he answering said to them, When evening is come, you say, Fine weather, for the sky is red;

3 and in the morning, A storm today, for the sky is red [and] lowering; you know [how] to discern the face of the sky, but you cannot read the signs of the times.

4 A wicked and adulterous generation seeks after a sign, and a sign shall not be given to it except the sign of Jonah. And he left them and went away.

Yeast of Pharisees and Sadducees

5 And when his disciples were come to the other side, they had forgotten to take bread.

6 And Yehoshua said to them, See and beware of the leaven of the Pharisees and Sadducees.

7 And they reasoned among themselves, saying, Because we have taken no bread.

8 And Yehoshua knowing [it] said, Why reason you among yourselves, O you of little faith, because you have taken no bread?

9 Do you not yet understand nor remember the five loaves of the five

thousand, and how many hand-baskets you took [up]

10 nor the seven loaves of the four thousand, and how many baskets you took [up]

11 How do you not understand that [it was] not concerning bread I said to you, Beware of the leaven of the Pharisees and Sadducees?

12 Then they comprehended that he did not speak of being beware of the leaven of bread, but of the doctrine of the Pharisees and Sadducees.

Yehoshua Heals Blind Man

Mark 8:22 And he comes to Beth-saida; and they bring him a blind man, and beseech him that he might touch him.

23 And taking hold of the hand of the blind man he led him forth out of the village, and having spit upon his eyes, he laid his hands upon him, and asked him if he beheld anything.

24 And having looked up, he said, I behold men, for I see [them] as trees, walking.

25 Then he laid his hands again upon his eyes, and he saw distinctly, and was restored and saw all things clearly.

26 And he sent him to his house, saying, Neither enter into the village, nor tell [it] to any one in the village.

Peter Acknowledges that Yehoshua is the Messiah

Matt 16:13 But when Yehoshua was come into the parts of Caesarea-Philippi, he asked of his disciples, saying, Who do men say that I the Son of man am?

14 And they said, Some, John the Baptist; and others, Elijah; and others again, Jeremiah or one of the prophets.

15 He says to them, But you, who do you say that I am?

16 And Simon Peter answering said, You are the Masiah, the Son of the living God.

17 And Yehoshua answering said to him, Blessed are you, Simon Bar- jona, for flesh and blood has not revealed [it] to you, but my Father who is in the heavens.

18 And I also, I say unto you that you are Peter, and on this the rock[17] I will build my assembly, and gates of hell [Hades] shall not prevail against it.

19 And I will give to you the keys of the kingdom of the heavens; and whatsoever you bind* upon the earth shall be [fut.] what was bound [perf.] in the heavens; and whatsoever you loose* on the earth shall be [fut.] what was loosed [perf.] in the heavens.[18]

20 Then he enjoined on his disciples that they should say to no man that he was the Masiah.

Yehoshua Foretells His Suffering

21 From that time Yehoshua began to show to his disciples that he must go away to Jerusalem, and suffer many things from the elders and chief priests and scribes, and be killed, and the third day be raised.

22 And Peter taking him to him began to rebuke him, saying, [god] be favorable to you, Lord; this shall in no way be unto you.

23 But turning round, he said to Peter, Get away behind me, Satan; you are an offence to me, for your mind is not on the things that are of the God, but on the things that are of men.

To Follow Masiah One must Deny Himself

24 Then Yehoshua said to his disciples, If any one desires to come after me, let him deny himself and take up his cross and follow me.

---

[17] Yehoshua Masiah is that "Rock"; see 1 Cor 10:4

[18] See nm30 & *New Testament*, by Williams

25 For whosoever shall desire to save his soul shall lose it; but whosoever shall lose his soul for my sake shall find it.

26 For what does a man profit, if he should gain the whole world and suffer the loss of his soul? or what shall a man give in exchange for his soul?

27 For the Son of man is about to come in the glory of his Father with his angels, and then he will render to each according to his doings.

Transfiguration

28 Truly I say unto you, There are some of those standing here that shall not taste of death at all until they shall have seen the Son of man coming in his kingdom.

Matt 17:1 And after six days Yehoshua takes with him Peter, and James, and John his brother, and brings them up into a high mountain apart.

2 And he was transfigured before them. And his face shone as the sun, and his garments became white as the light;

3 and lo, Moses and Elijah appeared to them talking with him.

4 And Peter answering said to Yehoshua, Lord, it is good we should be here. If you will, let us make here three tabernacles: for you one, and for Moses one, and one for Elijah.

5 While he was still speaking, behold, a bright cloud overshadowed them, and lo, a voice out of the cloud, saying, This is my beloved Son, in whom I have found my delight: hear him.

6 And the disciples hearing [it] fell upon their faces, and were greatly terrified.

7 And Yehoshua coming to [them] touched them, and said, Rise up, and be not terrified.

8 And lifting up their eyes, they saw no one but Yehoshua alone.

Elijah must come First

9 And as they descended from the mountain, Yehoshua charged them, saying, Tell the vision to no one, until the Son of man be risen up from among the dead.

10 And [his] disciples asked of him saying, Why then say the scribes that Elijah must first have come?

11 And he answering said to them, Elijah indeed comes first and will restore all things.

12 But I say unto you that Elijah has already come, and they have not known him, but have done unto him whatever they would. Thus also the Son of man is about to suffer from them.

13 Then the disciples understood that he spoke to them of John the Baptist.

Boy Healed

14 And when they came to the crowd, a man came to him, falling on his knees before him, and saying,

15 Lord, have mercy on my son, for he is lunatic, and suffers sorely; for often he falls into the fire and often into the water.

16 And I brought him to your disciples, and they were not able to heal him.

17 And Yehoshua answering said, O unbelieving and perverted generation, how long shall I be with you? how long shall I bear with you? Bring him here to me.

18 And Yehoshua rebuked him, and the daemon went out from him, and the boy was healed from that hour.

19 Then the disciples, coming to Yehoshua alone, said [to him] Why were not we able to cast him out?

20 And he says to them, Because of your unbelief; for truly I say unto you, If you have faith as a grain of mustard [seed] you shall say to this mountain, Be transported hence there, and it shall

transport itself; and nothing shall be impossible to you.

[21 But this kind does not go out but by prayer and fasting.]

Yehoshua Predicts Suffering Again

22 And while they abode in Galilee, Yehoshua said to them, The Son of man is about to be delivered up into the hands of men,

23 and they shall kill him; and the third day he shall be raised up. And they were greatly grieved.

Coin in Fish's Mouth to pay Taxes

24 And when they came to Capernaum, those who received the tax [didrachmas] came to Peter and said, Does your teacher not pay the tax [didrachmas]?

25 He says, Yes. And when he came into the house, Yehoshua anticipated him, saying, What do you think, Simon? the kings of the earth, from whom do they receive custom or tribute? from their own sons or from strangers?

26 Peter says to him, From strangers. Yehoshua said to him, Then are the sons free.

27 But that we may not be an offence to them, go to the sea and cast a hook, and take the first fish that comes up, and when you have opened its mouth you will find money [stater]; take that and give it to them for me and you.

Apostles Argue about Rank: Must become as a Child

Matt 18:1 In that hour the disciples came to Yehoshua saying, Who then is greatest in the kingdom of the heavens?

2 And Yehoshua having called a little child to him set it in their midst,

3 and said, Truly I say to you, Unless you are converted and become as little children, you will not at all enter into the kingdom of the heavens.

4 Whoever therefore shall humble himself as this little child, he is the greatest in the kingdom of the heavens;

5 and whosoever shall receive one such little child in my name, receives me.

Cut off your Hand if it Offends

6 But whosoever shall offend one of these little ones who believe in me, it were profitable for him that a great millstone had been hanged upon his neck and he be sunk in the depths of the sea.

7 Woe to the world because of offences! For it must needs be that offences come; yet woe to that man by whom the offence comes!

8 And if your hand or your foot offend you, cut it off and cast [it] from you; it is good for you to enter into life lame or maimed, [rather] than having two hands or two feet to be cast into the aeonian fire.

9 And if your eye offend you, pluck it out and cast [it] from you; it is good for you to enter into life one-eyed, [rather] than having two eyes to be cast into the hell [Gehenna] of fire.

10 See that you do not despise one of these little ones; for I say unto you that their angels in the heavens continually behold the face of my Father who is in the heavens.

Yehoshua came to Save the Lost

11 For the Son of man has come to save that which was lost.

12 What do you think? If a certain man should have a hundred sheep, and one of them be gone astray, does he not, leaving the ninety and nine on the mountains, go and seek the one that has gone astray?

13 And if it should come to pass that he find it, truly I say unto you, he rejoices more because of it than because of the ninety and nine not gone astray.

14 So it is not the will of your Father who is in the heavens that one of these little ones should perish.

If Your Brother Sin against You

15 But if your brother sin against you, go, reprove him between you and him alone. If he hear you, you have gained your brother.

16 But if he do not hear [you] take with you one or two besides, that every matter may stand upon the word of two witnesses or of three.

17 But if he will not listen to them, tell it to the assembly; and if also he will not listen to the assembly, let him be to you as one of the nations and a tax-gatherer.

When Two or Three are Come Together

18 Truly I say to you, Whatsoever you shall bind on the earth shall have been bound in heaven, and whatsoever you shall loose on the earth shall have been loosed in heaven.

19 Again I say to you, that if two of you shall agree on the earth concerning any matter, whatsoever it may be that they shall ask, it shall come to them from my Father who is in the heavens.

20 For where two or three are gathered together unto my name, there I am in the midst of them.

Forgiving Your Brother

21 Then Peter came to him and said, Lord, how often shall my brother sin against me and I forgive him? until seven times?

22 Yehoshua says to him, I say not to you until seven times, but until seventy times seven.

Parable of the Servant in Debt

23 For this cause the kingdom of the heavens has become like a king who would reckon with his servants.

24 And having begun to reckon, one debtor of ten thousand talents was brought to him.

25 But he not having anything to pay, [his] lord commanded him to be sold, and his wife, and his children, and everything that he had, and that payment should be made.

26 The servant therefore falling down did him homage, saying, Lord, have patience with me and I will pay you all.

27 And the lord of that servant, being moved with compassion, loosed him and forgave him the loan.

28 But that servant having gone out, found one of his fellow- servants who owed him a hundred denarii. And having seized him, he throttled him, saying, Pay [me] if you owest anything.

29 His fellow-servant therefore, having fallen down [at his feet] besought him, saying, Have patience with me, and I will pay you.

30 But he would not, but went away and cast him into prison, until he should pay what was owing.

31 But his fellow-servants, having seen what had taken place, were greatly grieved, and went and recounted to their lord all that had taken place.

32 Then his lord, having called him to him, says to him, Wicked servant! I forgave you all that debt because you besought me;

33 should not you also have had compassion on your fellow- servant, as I also had compassion on you?

34 And his lord being angry delivered him to the tormentors till he paid all that was owing to him.

35 Thus also my heavenly Father shall do to you if you forgive not from your hearts every one his brother. Time of Feast of Tabernacles

Yehoshua's own Brethren did not Believe in Him

John 7:2 Now the tabernacles,[19] the feast of the Jews, was near.

3 His brethren therefore said to him, Leave here and go into Judea, that your disciples also may see your works which you do;

4 for no one does anything in secret and himself seeks to be [known] in public. If you do these things, manifest yourself to the world:

5 for neither did his brethren believe on him.

6 Yehoshua therefore says to them, My time is not yet come, but your time is always ready.

7 The world cannot hate you, but it hates me, because I bear witness concerning it that its works are evil.

8 You, go up to this feast. I go not up to this feast, for my time is not yet fulfilled.

9 Having said these things to them he abode in Galilee.

Yehoshua's Brethren go to the Feast

10 But when his brethren had gone up, then he himself also went up to the feast, not openly, but as in secret.

11 The Jews therefore sought him at the feast, and said, Where is he?

12 And there was much murmuring concerning him among the crowds. Some said, He is a good [man] others said, No; but he deceives the crowd.

13 However, no one spoke openly concerning him on account of [their] fear of the Jews.

Yehoshua teaches in the Temple

14 But when it was now the middle of the feast, Yehoshua went up into the temple and taught.

15 The Jews therefore wondered, saying, How does this [man] know letters, having never learned?

16 Yehoshua therefore answered them and said, My doctrine is not mine, but that of him that has sent me.

17 If any one desire to practice his will, he shall know concerning the doctrine, whether it is of the God, or that I speak from myself.

18 He that speaks from himself seeks his own glory; but he that seeks the glory of him that has sent him, he is true, and unrighteousness is not in him.

19 Has not Moses given you the law, and no one of you practices the law? Why do you seek to kill me?

20 The crowd answered [and said] You have a daemon: who seeks to kill you?

21 Yehoshua answered and said to them, I have done one work, and you all wonder.

22 Therefore Moses gave you circumcision not that it is of Moses, but of the fathers, and you circumcise a man on Sabbath.

23 If a man receives circumcision on Sabbath, that the law of Moses may not be violated, are you angry with me because I have made a man entirely sound on Sabbath?

24 Judge not according to sight, but judge righteous judgment.

Jerusalem Talks About Yehoshua

25 Some therefore of those of Jerusalem said, Is not this he whom they seek to kill?

26 and behold, he speaks openly, and they say nothing to him. Have the rulers then indeed recognized that this is the Masiah?

---

[19] Three years of Ministry over with one-half year to go until Masiah' death

27 But [as to] this [man] we know where he is from? Now [as to] the Masiah, when he comes, no one knows where he is from.

Yehoshua: I am From Him

28 Yehoshua therefore cried out in the temple, teaching and saying, You both know me and you know from where I am; and I am not come of myself, but he that sent me is true, whom you do not know.

29 I know him, because I am from him, and he has sent me.

30 They sought therefore to take him; and no one laid his hand upon him, because his hour had not yet come.

31 But many of the crowd believed on him, and said, Will the Masiah, when he comes, do more signs than those which this [man] has done?

Guards Attempt to Arrest Yehoshua at the Feast

32 The Pharisees heard the crowd murmuring these things concerning him, and the Pharisees and the chief priests sent officers that they might take him.

33 Yehoshua therefore said, Yet a little while I am with you, and I go to him that has sent me.

34 You shall seek me and shall not find [me] and where I am you cannot come.

35 The Jews therefore said to one another, Where is he about to go that we shall not find him? Is he about to go to the dispersion among the Greeks, and teach the Greeks?

36 What word is this which he said, You shall seek me and shall not find [me] and where I am you cannot come?

Spiritual Water

37 In the last, the great day of the feast, Yehoshua stood and cried saying, If any one thirst, let him come to me and drink.

38 He that believes on me, as the scripture has said, out of his belly shall flow rivers of living water.

39 But this he said concerning the Spirit, which they that believed on him were about to receive; for the Spirit was not yet, because Yehoshua had not yet been glorified.

Jerusalem Argues: Is He or Is He Not the Messiah?

40 [Some] out of the crowd therefore, having heard this word, said, This is truly the prophet.

41 Others said, This is the Masiah. Others said, Does then the Masiah come out of Galilee?

42 Has not the scripture said that the Masiah comes of the seed of David, and from the village of Bethlehem, where David was?

43 There was a division therefore in the crowd on account of him.

44 But some of them desired to take him, but no one laid hands upon him.

Guards Report Back to the Chief Priests

45 The officers therefore came to the chief priests and Pharisees, and they said to them, Why have you not brought him?

46 The officers answered, No man has spoken as this man [speaks].

47 The Pharisees therefore answered them, Are you also deceived?

48 Has any one of the rulers believed on him, or of the Pharisees?

49 But this crowd, which does not know the law, are accursed.

50 Nicodemus says to them being one of themselves,

51 Does our law judge a man before it have first heard from himself, and know what he does?

52 They answered and said to him, Are you also of Galilee? Search and look, that no prophet arises out of Galilee.

53 And every one went to his home.

Woman Caught in Adultery

John 8:1 But Yehoshua went to the mount of Olives.

2 And early in the morning he came again into the temple, and all the people came to him; and he sat down and taught them.

3 And the scribes and the Pharisees bring [to him] a woman taken in adultery, and having set her in the midst,

4 they say to him, Teacher, this woman has been taken in the very act, committing adultery.

5 Now in the law Moses has commanded us to stone such; therefore, what do you say?

6 But this they said testing him, that they might have [something] to accuse him of. But Yehoshua, having stooped down, wrote with his finger on the ground.

7 But when they continued asking him, he lifted himself up and said to them, Let him that is without sin among you first cast the stone at her.

8 And again stooping down he wrote on the ground.

9 But they, having heard that went out one by one beginning from the elder ones until the last; and Yehoshua was left alone and the woman standing there.

10 And Yehoshua, lifting himself up and seeing no one but the woman, said to her, Woman, where are your accusers? Has no one condemned you?

11 And she said, No one, sir. And Yehoshua said to her, Neither do I condemn you: go, and sin no more.

Yehoshua the Light of the World

12 Again therefore Yehoshua spoke to them, saying, I am the light of the world; he that follows me shall not walk in darkness, but shall have the light of life.

Yehoshua: I am not Alone

13 The Pharisees therefore said to him, You bear witness concerning yourself; your witness is not true.

14 Yehoshua answered and said to them, Even if I bear witness concerning myself, my witness is true, because I know from where I came and where I go: but you know not from where I come and whither I go.

15 You judge according to the flesh, I judge no one.

16 And if also I judge, my judgment is true, because I am not alone, but I and the Father who has sent me.

17 And in your law too it is written that the testimony of two men is true:

18 I am [one] who bear witness concerning myself, and the Father who has sent me bears witness concerning me.

19 They said to him therefore, Where is your Father? Yehoshua answered, You know neither me nor my Father. If you had known me, you would have known also my Father.

20 These words he spoke in the treasury, teaching in the temple; and no one took him, for his hour was not yet come.

One Who Sent Yehoshua is with Him

21 He said therefore again to them, I go away, and you shall seek me, and shall die in your sin; where I go you cannot come.

22 The Jews therefore said, Will he kill himself, that he says, Where I go you cannot come?

23 And he said to them, You are from beneath; I am from above. You are of this world; I am not of this world.

24 I said therefore to you, that you shall die in your sins; for unless you shall believe that I am he, you shall die in your sins.

25 They said therefore to him, Who are you? [and] Yehoshua said to them, that which I said to you from the first.

26 I have many things to say and to judge concerning you, but he that has sent me is true, and I, what I have heard from him, these things I say to the world.

27 They knew not that he spoke to them of the Father.

28 Yehoshua therefore said to them, When you shall have lifted up the Son of man, then you shall know that I am he, and that I do nothing of myself, but as the Father has taught me I speak these things.

29 And he that has sent me is with me; he has not left me alone, because I do always the things that are pleasing to him.

30 As he spoke these things many believed on him.

Truth will set you Free

31 Yehoshua therefore said to the Jews who believed him, If you abide in my word, you are truly my disciples;

32 and you shall know the truth, and the truth shall set you free.

33 They answered him, We are Abraham's seed, and have never been under bondage to any one; how can you say, You shall become free?

34 Yehoshua answered them, Truly, truly, I say to you, Every one that practices sin is the servant of sin.

35 Now the servant abides not in the house into the aeon: the son abides into the aeon.

36 If therefore the Son shall set you free, you shall be really free.

37 I know that you are Abraham's seed; but you seek to kill me, because my word has no room in you.

38 I speak what I have seen with my Father, and you then do what you have seen with your father.

Unbeliever's Father is the Devil

39 They answered and said to him, Abraham is our father. Yehoshua says to them, If you were Abraham's children, you would do the works of Abraham;

40 but now you seek to kill me, a man who has spoken the truth to you, which I have heard from the God: this Abraham did not do.

41 You do the works of your father. They said [therefore] to him, We are not born of fornication; we have one father, the God.

42 Yehoshua said to them, If the God were your father you would have loved me, for I came forth from the God and am come [from him] for neither am I come of myself, but he has sent me.

43 Why do you not know my speech? Because you cannot hear my word.

44 You are of the devil as your father, and you desire to do the lusts of your father. He was a murderer from the beginning, and has not stood in the truth, because there is no truth in him. When he speaks falsehood, he speaks of what is his own; for he is a liar and its father:

45 and because I speak the truth, you do not believe me.

46 Which of you convicts me of sin? If I speak truth, why do you not believe me?

47 He that is of the God hears the words of the God: therefore you hear [them] not, because you are not of the God.

Before Abraham, Yehoshua Existed

48 The Jews answered and said to him, Are we not right that you are a Samaritan and have a daemon?

49 Yehoshua answered, I have not a daemon; but I honor my Father, and you dishonor me.

50 But I do not seek my own glory: there is he that seeks and judges.

51 Truly, truly, I say unto you, If any one shall keep my word, he shall not in the aeon see death.

52 The Jews therefore said to him, Now we know that you have a daemon. Abraham has died, and the prophets, and you say, If any one keep my word, he shall not in the aeon taste death.

53 Are you greater than our father Abraham, who has died? and the prophets have died: whom are you making yourself?

54 Yehoshua answered, If I glorify myself, my glory is nothing: it is my Father who glorifies me, of whom you say, He is our God.

55 And you know him not; but I know him; and if I said, I know him not, I would be like you, a liar. But I know him, and I keep his word.

56 Your father Abraham exulted in that he should see my day, and he saw and rejoiced.

57 The Jews therefore said to him, You have not yet fifty years, and have you seen Abraham?

58 Yehoshua said to them, Truly, truly, I say unto you, Before Abraham was, I existed.

59 They took up therefore stones that they might cast [them] at him; but Yehoshua hid himself and went out of the temple, [going through the midst of them, and thus passed on]

Heals the Blind and Gives Light to the World

John 9:1 And as he passed on, he saw a man blind from birth.

2 And his disciples asked him, saying, Rabbi, who sinned, this [man] or his parents, that he should be born blind?

3 Yehoshua answered, Neither has this [man] sinned nor his parents, but that the works of the God should be manifested in him.

4 I must work the works of him that has sent me while it is day. the night is coming, when no one can work.

5 As long as I am in the world, I am the light of the world.

6 Having said these things, he spat on the ground and made mud of the spittle, and put the mud, as ointment, on his eyes.

7 And he said to him, Go, wash in the pool of Siloam, which is interpreted, Sent. He went therefore and washed, and came seeing.

8 The neighbors therefore, and those who used to see him before, that he was a beggar, said, Is not this he that was sitting and begging?

9 Some said, It is he; others said, No, but he is like him: he said, It is I.

10 They said therefore to him, How have your eyes been opened?

11 He answered [and said], A man called Yehoshua made mud and anointed mine eyes, and said to me, Go to Siloam and wash: and having gone and washed, I saw.

12 They said therefore to him, Where is he? He says, I do not know.

13 They bring him who was before blind to the Pharisees.

14 Now it was Sabbath when Yehoshua made the mud and opened his eyes.

15 The Pharisees therefore also again asked him how he received his sight.

And he said to them, He put mud upon mine eyes, and I washed, and I see.

16 Some of the Pharisees therefore said, This man is not from the God, for he does not keep the Sabbath. Others said, How can a sinful man perform such signs? And there was a division among them.

17 They say therefore again to the blind [man] What do you say of him, that he has opened your eyes? And he said, He is a prophet.

18 The Jews therefore did not believe concerning him that he was blind and had received sight, until they had called the parents of him that had received sight.

19 And they asked them saying, This is your son, of whom you say that he was born blind: how then does he now see?

20 His parents answered [them] and said, We know that this is our son, and that he was born blind;

21 but how he now sees we do not know, or who has opened his eyes we do not know. He is of age: ask him; he will speak concerning himself.

22 His parents said these things because they feared the Jews, for the Jews had already agreed that if any one acknowledged him [to be the] Masiah, he should be excommunicated from the synagogue.

23 On this account his parents said, He is of age: ask him.

24 They called therefore a second time the man who had been blind, and said to him, Give glory to the God: we know that this man is sinful.

25 He answered therefore, If he is sinful I know not. One thing I know, that, being blind [before] now I see.

26 And they said to him again, What did he do to you? how did he open your eyes?

27 He answered them, I told you already and you did not hear: why do you desire to hear again? do you also wish to become his disciples?

28 They railed at him, and said, You are his disciple, but we are disciples of Moses.

29 We know that the God spoke to Moses; but [as to] this [man] we know not where he is from.

30 The man answered and said to them, Now in this is a wonderful thing, that you do not know where he is from, and he has opened mine eyes.

31 [But] we know that the God does not hear sinners; but if any one be God-fearing and do his will, him he hears.

32 Since time was, it has not been heard that any one opened the eyes of one born blind.

33 If this [man] were not of God he would be able to do anything.

34 They answered and said to him, You have been wholly born in sins, and you teach us? And they cast him out.

35 Yehoshua heard that they had cast him out, and having found him, he said to him, You, do you believe on the Son of the God?

36 He answered and said, And who is he, Lord, that I may believe on him?

37 And Yehoshua said to him, You have both seen him, and he that speaks with you is he.

38 And he said, I believe, Lord: and he did him homage.

39 And Yehoshua said, For judgment I have come into this world, that they which see not may see, and they which see may become blind.

40 And [some] of the Pharisees who were with him heard these things, and they said to him, Are we blind also?

41 Yehoshua said to them, If you were blind you would not have sin; but now you say, We see, your sin remains.

Yehoshua the True Shepherd and Door

John 10:1 Truly, truly, I say to you, He that enters not in by the door to the fold of the sheep, but mounts up elsewhere, he is a thief and a robber;

2 but he that enters in by the door is the shepherd of the sheep.

3 To him the doorkeeper opens; and the sheep hear his voice; and he calls his own sheep by name, and leads them out.

4 When he has put forth all his own, he goes before them, and the sheep follow him, because they know his voice.

5 But they will not follow a stranger, but will flee from him, because they know not the voice of strangers.

6 This parable spoke Yehoshua to them, but they did not know what it was of which he spoke to them.

7 Yehoshua therefore said again to them, Truly, truly, I say to you, I am the door of the sheep.

8 All whoever came before me are thieves and robbers; but the sheep did not hear them.

9 I am the door: if any one enter in by me, he shall be saved, and shall go in and shall go out and shall find pasture.

10 The thief comes not but that he may steal, and kill, and destroy: I am come that they might have life, and might have it abundantly.

11 I am the good shepherd. The good shepherd lays down his soul for the sheep:

12 but he who serves for wages, and who is not the shepherd, whose own the sheep are not, sees the wolf coming, and leaves the sheep and flees; and the wolf seizes them and scatters the sheep.

13 Now he who serves for wages flees because he serves for wages, and is not himself concerned about the sheep.

14 I am the good shepherd; and I know those that are mine, and am known of those that are mine,

15 as the Father knows me and I know the Father; and I lay down my soul for the sheep.

16 And I have other sheep which are not of this fold: those also I must bring, and they shall hear my voice; and there shall be one flock, one shepherd.

17 On this account the Father loves me, because I lay down my soul that I may take it again.

18 No one takes it from me, but I lay it down of myself. I have authority to lay it down and I have authority to take it again. I have received this commandment of my Father.

Jews Divided over Healing of the Blind

John 10:19 There was a division again among the Jews on account of these words;

20 but many of them said, He has a daemon and raves; why do you hear him?

21 Others said, These sayings are not [those] of one that is possessed by a daemon. Can a daemon open blind people's eyes?

Yehoshua sets out to Jerusalem

Luke 9:51 When the days drew near for him to be taken up, he set his face to go to Jerusalem.

52 And he sent messengers before his face. And having gone they entered into a village of the Samaritans that they might make ready for him.

53 And they did not receive him, because his face was [turned as] going to Jerusalem.

54 And his disciples James and John seeing it said, Lord, wish you that we speak that fire come down from heaven and consume them, as also Elijah did?

55 But turning he rebuked them [and said, You know not of what spirit you are]

56 And they went to another village.

Ten lepers Healed

Luke 17:11 And it came to pass as he was going up to Jerusalem, that he passed through the midst of Samaria and Galilee.

12 And as he entered into a certain village ten leprous men met him, who stood afar off.

13 And they lifted up [their] voice saying, Yehoshua, Master, have compassion on us.

14 And seeing [them] he said to them, Go, show yourselves to the priests. And it came to pass as they were going they were cleansed.

15 And one of them, seeing that he was cured, turned back, glorifying the God with a loud voice,

16 and fell on [his] face at his feet giving him thanks: and he was a Samaritan.

17 And Yehoshua answering said, Were not the ten cleansed? but the nine, where [are they]

18 There have not been found to return and give glory to the God except this stranger.

19 And he said to him, Rise up and go your way: your faith has made you well.

Yehoshua Sends Disciples Out, Two by Two

Luke 10:1 Now after these things the Lord appointed seventy others also, and sent them two and two before his face into every city and place where he himself was about to come.

2 And he said to them, The harvest indeed [is] great, but the workmen few; pray therefore the Lord of the harvest that he may send out workmen into his harvest.

3 Go: behold I send you forth as lambs in the midst of wolves.

4 Carry neither purse nor scrip nor sandals, and salute no one on the way.

5 And into whatsoever house you enter, first say, Peace to this house.

6 And if a son of peace be there, your peace shall rest upon it; but if not it shall return to you again.

7 And in the same house abide, eating and drinking such things as they have; for the workman is worthy of his hire. Remove not from house to house.

8 And into whatsoever city you may enter and they receive you, eat what is set before you,

9 and heal the sick in it, and say to them, The kingdom of the God is come near to you.

10 But into whatsoever city you may have entered and they do not receive you, go out into its streets and say,

11 Even the dust of your city, which cleaves to us on the feet, do we shake off against you; but know this, that the kingdom of the God is come nigh.

12 I say to you that it shall be more tolerable for Sodom in that day than for that city.

13 Woe to you, Chorazin! woe to you, Bethsaida! for if the works of power which have taken place in you had taken place in Tyre and Sidon, they had long ago repented sitting in sackcloth and ashes.

14 But it shall be more tolerable for Tyre and Sidon in the judgment than for you.

15 And you, Capernaum, who have been raised up to heaven, shall be brought down even to hell [Hades].

16 He that hears you hears me; and he that rejects you rejects me; and he that rejects me rejects him that sent me.

Yehoshua: I see Satan fall like Lightning from Heaven

17 And the seventy returned with joy, saying, Lord, even the daemons are subject to us through your name.

18 And he said to them, I am seeing Satan as lightning falling out of heaven.

19 Behold, I give you the power of treading upon serpents and scorpions and over all the power of the enemy, and nothing shall in anyway injure you.

20 Yet in this rejoice not, that the spirits are subjected to you, but rejoice that your names are written in the heavens.

No One Knows the Father Except the Son and to whom the Son Chooses to Reveal

21 In the same hour Yehoshua rejoiced in spirit and said, I praise you, Father, Lord of the heaven and of the earth, that you have hid these things from the wise and prudent, and have revealed them to babes: yes, Father, for thus has it been well-pleasing in your sight.

22 All things have been delivered to me by my Father, and no one knows who the Son is but the Father, and who the Father is but the Son, and he to whomsoever the Son is pleased to reveal him.

23 And having turned to the disciples privately he said, Blessed are the eyes which see the things that you see.

24 For I say to you that many prophets and kings have desired to see the things which you behold, and did not see [them] and to hear the things which you hear, and did not hear [them]

Come to Yehoshua all who are Weary and Burdened

Matt 11:28 Come to me, all you who labor and are burdened, and I will give you rest.

29 Take my yoke upon you, and learn from me; for I am meek and lowly in heart; and you shall find rest to your souls;

30 for my yoke is easy, and my burden is light.

Parable of the Good Samaritan

Luke 10:25 And behold, a certain lawyer stood up testting him, and saying, Teacher, having done what, shall I inherit aeonian life?

26 And he said to him, What is written in the law? how do you read it?

27 But he answering said, You shall love the Lord your God with all your heart, and with all your soul, and with all your strength, and with all your understanding; and your neighbor as yourself.

28 And he said to him, You have answered right: this do and you shall live.

29 But he, desirous of justifying himself, said to Yehoshua, And who is my neighbor?

30 And Yehoshua replying said, A certain man descended from Jerusalem to Jericho and fell into [the hands of] robbers, who also, having stripped him and inflicted wounds, went away leaving him in a half-dead state.

31 And a certain priest happened to go down that way, and seeing him, passed on on the opposite side;

32 and in like manner also a Levite, being at the spot, came and looked [at him] and passed on the opposite side.

33 But a certain Samaritan journeying came to him, and seeing him was moved with compassion,

34 and came up [to him] and bound up his wounds, pouring in oil and wine; and having put him on his own beast, took him to the inn and took care of him.

35 And on the next day [as he left] taking out two denarii he gave them to the innkeeper, and said to him, Take care of him, and whatsoever you shall expend more, I will render to you on my coming back.

36 Which [now] of these three seems to you to have been neighbor of him who fell into [the hands of] the robbers?

37 And he said, He that showed him mercy. And Yehoshua said to him, Go, and do you likewise.

Spiritual Work Better Than Physical

38 And it came to pass as they went that he entered into a certain village; and a certain woman, Martha by name, received him into her house.

39 And she had a sister called Mary, who also, having sat down at the feet of Yehoshua was listening to his word.

40 Now Martha was distracted with much serving, and coming up she said, Lord, do you not care that my sister has left me to serve alone? Speak to her therefore that she may help me.

41 But Yehoshua answering said to her, Martha, Martha, you are concerned and troubled about many things;

42 but there is need of one, and Mary has chosen the good part, the which shall not be taken from her.

How to Pray

Luke 11:1 And it came to pass as he was in a certain place praying, when he ceased, one of his disciples said to him, Lord, teach us to pray, even as John also taught his disciples.

2 And he said to them, When you pray, say, Father, your name be hallowed; your kingdom come;

3 give us our needed bread for each day;

4 and forgive us our sins, for we also forgive to every one indebted to us; and lead us not into temptation.

Parable of Persistence

5 And he said to them, Who among you shall have a friend, and shall go to him at midnight and say to him, Friend, let me have three loaves,

6 since a friend of mine on a journey is come to me, and I have nothing to set before him;

7 and he within answering should say, Do not disturb me; the door is already shut, and my children are with me in bed; I cannot rise up to give it you?

8 – I say to you, Although he will not get up and give [them] to him because he is his friend, because of his shamelessness [boldness to ask], at any rate, he will rise and give him as many as he wants.

9 And I say to you, Ask, and it shall be given to you; seek, and you shall find; knock, and it shall be opened to you.

10 For every one that asks receives; and he that seeks finds; and to him that knocks it will be opened.

11 But of whom of you that is a father shall a son ask bread, and [the father] shall give him a stone? or also a fish, and instead of a fish shall give him a serpent?

12 or if also he shall ask an egg, shall give him a scorpion?

13 If therefore you, being evil, know how to give good gifts to your children, how much rather shall the Father who is of heaven give the Holy Spirit to them that ask him?

Unbelieving Jews Not Yehoshua's Sheep

John 10:22 Now the feast of the dedication was celebrating at Jerusalem, and it was winter.

23 And Yehoshua walked in the temple in the porch of Solomon.

24 The Jews therefore surrounded him, and said to him, Until when do you hold our soul in suspense? If you are the Masiah, say [so] to us openly.

25 Yehoshua answered them, I told you, and you do not believe. The works which I do in my Father's name, these bear witness concerning me:

26 but you do not believe, for you are not of my sheep, as I told you.

27 My sheep hear my voice, and I know them, and they follow me;

28 and I give them aeonian life; and they in no way shall perish into the aeon [age], and no one shall seize them out of my hand.

Yehoshua Masiah's Father Greater than all: "I and the Father are One"

29 My Father who has given [them] to me is greater than all, and no one can seize out of the hand of my Father.

30 I and the Father are one.

31 The Jews therefore again took stones that they might stone him.

32 Yehoshua answered them, Many good works have I shown you of my Father; for which work of them do you stone me?

33 The Jews answered him, For a good work we stone you not, but for blasphemy, and because you, being a man, make yourself God.

34 Yehoshua answered them, Is it not written in your law, I said, You are gods ["elohim" (Psalm 82:6)]?

35 If he called them gods to whom the word of the God came and the scripture cannot be broken,

36 do you say of him whom the Father has sanctified and sent into the world, You are blasphemous, because I said, I am Son of the God?

37 If I do not the works of my Father, believe me not;

38 but if I do, even if you believe me not, believe the works, that you may know [and believe] that the Father is in me and I in him.

39 They sought therefore again to take him; and he went away from out of their hand

Yehoshua withdraws After Another Attempt to Seize Him

40 and departed again beyond the Jordan to the place where John was baptizing at the first: and he abode there.

41 And many came to him, and said, John did no sign; but all things which John said of this [man] were true.

42 And many believed on him there.

Are only a few Saved?

Luke 13:22 And he went through one city and village after another, teaching, and journeying to Jerusalem.

23 And one said to him, Sir, [are] such as are to be saved few in number? But he said unto them,

24 Strive with earnestness to enter in through the narrow door, for many, I say to you, will seek to enter in and will not be able.

25 From the time that the master of the house shall have risen up and shall have shut the door, and you shall begin to stand outside and to knock at the door, saying, Lord, open to us; and he answering shall say to you, I know you not who you are:

26 then shall you begin to say, We have eaten in your presence and drunk, and you have taught in our streets;

27 and he shall say, I tell you, I do not know who you are; depart from me, all you workers of iniquity.

28 There shall be the weeping and the gnashing of teeth, when you shall see

Abraham and Isaac and Jacob and all the prophets in the kingdom of the God, but yourselves cast out.

29 And they shall come from east and west, and from north and south, and shall lie down at table in the kingdom of the God.

30 And behold, there are last who shall be first, and there are first who shall be last.

Herod Wants to Kill Masiah

31 The same hour certain Pharisees came up, saying to him, Get out, and go away, for Herod is desirous to kill you.

32 And he said to them, Go, tell that fox, Behold, I cast out daemons and accomplish cures today and tomorrow, and the third [day] I am perfected;

33 but I must walk today and tomorrow and the [day] following, for it must be that no prophet shall perish outside of Jerusalem.

Lament over Jerusalem

34 Jerusalem, Jerusalem, the [city] that kills the prophets and stones those that are sent unto her, how often would I have gathered your children together, as a hen her brood under her wings, and you would not.

35 Behold, your house is left unto you; and I say unto you, that you shall not see me until it come that you say, Blessed [is] he that comes in the name of the Lord.

Man Healed, Healing on the Sabbath

Luke 14:1 And it came to pass, as he went into the house of one of the rulers, [who was] of the Pharisees, to eat bread on the Sabbath, that they were watching him.

2 And behold, there was a certain dropsical [man] before him.

3 And Yehoshua answering spoke unto the doctors of the law and Pharisees, saying, Is it lawful to heal on the Sabbath?

4 But they were silent. And taking him he healed him and let him go.

5 And answering he said to them, Of which of you shall an donkey or ox fall into a well, that he does not straightway pull him up on the Sabbath day?

6 And they were not able to answer him to these things.

Parable of Places of Honor

7 And he spoke a parable to those that were invited, remarking how they chose out the first places, saying to them,

8 When you are invited by any one to a wedding, do not lay yourself down in the first place at table, lest perhaps a more honorable than you be invited by him,

9 and he who invited you and him come and say to you, Give place to this [man] and then you begin with shame to take the last place.

10 But when you have been invited, go and put yourself down in the last place, that when he who has invited you comes, he may say to you, Friend, go up higher: then shall you have honor before all that are lying at table with you;

11 for every one that exalts himself shall be abased, and he that abases himself shall be exalted.

Invite All to your Supper

12 And he said also to him that had invited him, When you make a dinner or a supper, call not your friends, nor your brethren, nor your kinsfolk, nor rich neighbors, lest it may be they also should invite you in return, and a recompense be made you.

13 But when you make a feast, call poor, crippled, lame, blind:

14 and you shall be blessed; for they have not [the means] to recompense you; for it shall be recompensed you in the resurrection of the just.

Parable of the Great Banquet

15 And one of those that were lying at table with [them] hearing these things, said to him, Blessed [is] he who shall eat bread in the kingdom of the God.

16 And he said to him, A certain man made a great supper and invited many.

17 And he sent his servant at the hour of supper to say to those who were invited, Come, for already all things are ready.

18 And all began, without exception, to excuse themselves. The first said to him, I have bought land, and I must go out and see it; I pray you hold me for excused.

19 And another said, I have bought five yoke of oxen, and I go to prove them; I ask you to excuse me.

20 And another said, I have married a wife, and on this account I cannot come.

21 And the servant came up and brought back word of these things to his lord. Then the master of the house, in anger, said to his servant, Go out quickly into the streets and lanes of the city, and bring here the poor and crippled and lame and blind.

22 And the servant said, Sir, it is done as you have commanded, and there is still room.

23 And the lord said to the servant, Go out into the ways and fences and compel to come in, that my house may be filled;

24 for I say to you, that not one of those men who were invited shall taste of my supper.

Count the Cost to Follow Masiah

25 And great crowds went with him; and, turning round, he said to them,

26 If any man come to me, and shall not hate his own father and mother, and wife, and children, and brothers, and sisters, yes, and his own soul too, he cannot be my disciple;

27 and whoever does not carry his cross and come after me cannot be my disciple.

28 For which of you, desirous of building a tower, does not first sit down and count the cost, if he has what [is needed] to complete it;

29 in order that, having laid the foundation of it, and not being able to finish it, all who see it do not begin to mock him,

30 saying, This man began to build and was not able to finish?

31 Or what king, going on his way to engage in war with another king, does not, sitting down first, take counsel whether he is able with ten thousand to meet him coming against him with twenty thousand?

32 and if not, while he is yet far off, having sent an embassy, he asks for terms of peace.

33 Thus then every one of you who forsakes not all that is his own cannot be my disciple.

Salt of the Earth

34 Salt [then] [is] good, but if the salt also has become flavorless, wherewith shall it be seasoned?

35 It is proper neither for land nor for dung; it is cast out. He that hath ears to hear, let him hear.

Lost Sheep

Luke 15:1 And all the tax-gatherers and the sinners were coming near to him to hear him;

2 and the Pharisees and the scribes murmured, saying, This [man] receives sinners and eats with them.

3 And he spoke to them this parable, saying,

4 What man of you having a hundred sheep, and having lost one of them, does not leave the ninety and nine in the

wilderness and go after that which is lost, until he find it?

5 and having found it, he lays it upon his own shoulders, rejoicing;

6 and being come to the house, calls together the friends and the neighbors, saying to them, Rejoice with me, for I have found my lost sheep.

7 I say unto you, that thus there shall be joy in heaven for one repenting sinner, [more] than for ninety and nine righteous who have no need of repentance

Lost Coin

8 Or, what woman having ten drachmas, if she lose one drachma, does not light a lamp and sweep the house and seek carefully till she find it?

9 and having found it she calls together the friends and neighbors, saying, Rejoice with me, for I have found the drachma which I had lost.

10 Thus, I say unto you, there is joy before the angels of the God for one repenting sinner.

Lost Son

11 And he said, A certain man had two sons;

12 and the younger of them said to his father, Father, give to me the share of the property that falls [to me] And he divided to them what he was possessed of.

13 And after not many days the younger son gathering all together went away into a country a long way off, and there dissipated his property, living in debauchery.

14 But when he had spent all there arose a violent famine throughout that country, and he began to be in want.

15 And he went and joined himself to one of the citizens of that country, and he sent him into his fields to feed swine.

16 And he longed to fill his belly with the husks which the swine were eating; and no one gave to him.

17 And coming to himself, he said, How many hired servants of my father's have abundance of bread, and I perish here by famine.

18 I will rise up and go to my father, and I will say to him, Father, I have sinned against heaven and before you;

19 I am no longer worthy to be called your son: make me as one of your hired servants.

20 And he rose up and went to his own father. But while he was yet a long way off, his father saw him, and was moved with compassion, and ran, and fell upon his neck, and covered him with kisses.

21 And the son said to him, Father, I have sinned against heaven and before you; I am no longer worthy to be called your son.

22 But the father said to his servants, Bring out the best robe and clothe him in it and put a ring on his hand and sandals on his feet;

23 and bring the fatted calf and kill it, and let us eat and make merry:

24 for this my son was dead and has come to life, was lost and has been found. And they began to make merry.

25 And his elder son was in the field; and as, coming [up] he drew near to the house, he heard music and dancing.

26 And having called one of the servants, he inquired what these things might be.

27 And he said to him, Your brother is come, and your father has killed the fatted calf because he has received him safe and well.

28 But he became angry and would not go in. And his father went out and besought him.

29 But he answering said to his father, Behold, so many years I serve you, and never have I transgressed a commandment of yours; and to me have you never given a kid that I might make merry with my friends:

30 but when this your son, who has devoured your substance with harlots, is come, you have killed for him the fatted calf.

31 But he said to him, Child, you are ever with me, and all that is mine is yours.

32 But it was right to make merry and rejoice, because this your brother was dead and has come to life again, and was lost and has been found.

Dishonest Manager

Luke 16:1 And he said also to [his] disciples, There was a certain rich man who had a steward, and he was accused to him as wasting his goods.

2 And having called him, he said to him, What [is] this that I hear of you? give the reckoning of your stewardship, for you can be no longer steward.

3 And the steward said within himself, What shall I do; for my lord is taking the stewardship from me? I am not able to dig; I am ashamed to beg.

4 I know what I will do, that when I shall have been removed from the stewardship I may be received into their houses.

5 And having called to him each one of the debtors of his own lord, he said to the first, How much do you owe my lord?

6 And he said, A hundred baths of oil. And he said to him, Take your writing and sit down quickly and write fifty.

7 Then he said to another, And you, how much do you owe? And he said, A hundred measures of wheat. And he says to him, Take your writing and write eighty.

8 And the lord praised the unrighteous steward because he had done prudently. For the sons of this world are, for their own generation, more prudent than the sons of light.

9 And I say to you, Make to yourselves friends away from the mammon of unrighteousness [thus make friends of those of righteousness], that when it [way of mammon] fails you may be received into the aeonian tabernacles.

10 He that is faithful in the least is faithful also in much; and he that is unrighteous in the least is unrighteous also in much.

11 If therefore you have not been faithful in the unrighteous mammon, who shall entrust to you the true?

12 and if you have not been faithful in that which is another's, who shall give to you your own?

13 No servant can serve two masters, for either he will hate the one and will love the other, or he will cleave to the one and despise the other. You cannot serve God and mammon.

Man's Value v. God's Value

14 And the Pharisees also, who were covetous, heard all these things, and mocked him.

15 And he said to them, You are they who justify themselves before men, but the God knows your hearts; for what among men is highly thought of is an abomination before the God.

Law and Prophets Proclaim Until John

16 The law and the prophets [were] until John: from that time the good news of the kingdom of the God is announced, and every one forces his way into it.

17 But it is easier that the heaven and the earth should pass away than that one tittle of the law should fail.

18 Every one who puts away his wife and marries another commits adultery;

and every one that marries one put away from a husband commits adultery.

Rich Man and Lazarus

19 Now there was a rich man and he was clothed in purple and fine linen, making good cheer in splendor every day.

20 And [there was] a poor man, by name Lazarus, [who] was laid at his gateway full of sores,

21 and desiring to be filled with the crumbs which fell from the table of the rich man; but the dogs also coming licked his sores.

22 And it came to pass that the poor man died, and that he was carried away by the angels into the bosom of Abraham. And the rich man also died and was buried.

23 And in hell [Hades] lifting up his eyes, being in torments, he sees Abraham afar off, and Lazarus in his bosom.

24 And he crying out said, Father Abraham, have compassion on me, and send Lazarus that he may dip the tip of his finger in water and cool my tongue, for I am suffering in this flame.

25 But Abraham said, Child, recollect that you have fully received your good things in your lifetime, and likewise Lazarus evil things. But now he is comforted here, and you are in suffering.

26 And besides all this, between us and you a great chasm is fixed, so that those who desire to pass hence to you cannot, nor do they who [desire to cross] from there pass over unto us.

27 And he said, I beseech you then, father, that you would send him to the house of my father,

28 for I have five brothers, so that he may earnestly testify to them, that they also may not come to this place of torment.

29 But Abraham says to him, They have Moses and the prophets: let them hear them.

30 But he said, No, father Abraham, but if one from the dead should go to them, they will repent.

31 And he said to him, If they hear not Moses and the prophets, not even if one rise from among the dead will they be persuaded.

Yehoshua Teaches Forgiveness

Luke 17:1 And he said to his disciples, It cannot be but that offences come, but woe [to him] by whom they come!

2 It would be [more] profitable for him if a millstone were hanged about his neck and he cast into the sea, than that he should be a snare to one of these little ones.

3 Take heed to yourselves: if your brother should sin, rebuke him; and if he should repent, forgive him.

4 And if he should sin against you seven times in the day, and seven times should return to you, saying, I repent, you shall forgive him.

5 And the apostles said to the Lord, Give more faith to us.

6 But the Lord said, If you have faith as a grain of mustard [seed] you had said to this mulberry tree, Be you rooted up, and be you planted in the sea, and it would have obeyed you.

Servant's Duty

7 But which of you [is there] who, having a servant ploughing or shepherding, when he comes in out of the field, will say, Come and lie down immediately to the table?

8 But will he not say to him, Prepare what I shall sup on, and gird yourself and serve me that I may eat and drink; and after that you shall eat and drink?

9 Is he thankful to the servant because he has done what was ordered? I judge not.

10 Thus you also, when you shall have done all things that have been ordered you, say, We are unprofitable servants; we have done what it was our duty to do.

Coming of the Kingdom

Luke 17:20 And having been asked by the Pharisees, When is the kingdom of the God coming? he answered them and said, The kingdom of the God does not come with meticulous observation;

21 nor shall they say, Lo here, or, Lo there; for behold, the kingdom of the God is in the midst of you.

22 And he said to the disciples, Days are coming, when you shall desire to see one of the days of the Son of man, and shall not see it

23 And they will say to you, Lo here, or Lo there; go not, nor follow [them]

24 For as the lightning shines which lightens from [one end] under heaven to [the other end] under heaven, thus shall the Son of man be in his day.

25 But first he must suffer many things and be rejected of this generation.

26 And as it took place in the days of Noah, thus also shall it be in the days of the Son of man:

27 they ate, they drank, they married, they were given in marriage, until the day that Noah entered into the ark, and the flood came and destroyed all [of them]

28 and in like manner as took place in the days of Lot: they ate, they drank, they bought, they sold, they planted, they built;

29 but on the day that Lot went out from Sodom, it rained fire and sulphur from heaven, and destroyed all [of them]

30 after this [manner] shall it be in the day that the Son of man is revealed.

31 In that day, he who shall be on the housetop, and his stuff in the house, let him not go down to take it away; and he that is in the field, let him likewise not return back.

32 Remember the wife of Lot.

33 Whosoever shall seek to save his soul shall lose it, and whosoever shall lose it shall preserve it.

34 I say to you, In that night there shall be two [men] upon one bed; one shall be seized and the other shall be let go.

35 Two [women] shall be grinding together; the one shall be seized and the other shall be let go.

36 [Two men shall be in the field; the one shall be seized and the other let go]

37 And answering they say to him, Where, Lord? And he said to them, Where the body [is] there the eagles will be gathered together.

Parable of the Persistent Widow

Luke 18:1 And he spoke also a parable to them to the purport that they should always pray and not faint,

2 saying, There was a judge in a city, not fearing the God and not respecting man:

3 and there was a widow in that city, and she came to him, saying, Avenge me of mine adverse party.

4 And he would not for a time; but afterwards he said within himself, If even I fear not the God and respect not man,

5 at any rate because this widow annoys me I will avenge her, that she may not by perpetually coming completely harass me.

6 And the Lord said, Hear what the unjust judge says.

7 And shall not the God at all avenge his elect, who cry to him day and night, and he bears long as to them?

8 I say unto you that he will avenge them speedily. But when the Son of man comes, shall he indeed find faith on the earth?

Everyone who exalts himself will be humbled

9 And he spoke also this parable to some, who trusted in themselves that they were righteous and looked down all the rest [of men]:

10 Two men went up into the temple to pray; the one a Pharisee, and the other a tax-gatherer.

11 The Pharisee, standing, prayed thus to himself: God, I thank you that I am not as the rest of men, rapacious, unjust, adulterous, or even as this tax-gatherer.

12 I fast twice in the week, I tithe everything I gain.

13 And the tax-gatherer, standing afar off, would not lift up even his eyes to heaven, but smote upon his breast, saying, O God, have compassion on me, the sinner.

14 I say unto you, This [man] went down to his house justified rather than that [other] For every one who exalts himself shall be humbled, and he that humbles himself shall be exalted.

Parable of the Vineyard Workers

Matt 20:1 For the kingdom of the heavens is like a householder who went out with the early morn to hire workmen for his vineyard.

2 And having agreed with the workmen for a denarius the day, he sent them into his vineyard.

3 And having gone out about the third hour, he saw others standing in the market-place idle;

4 and to them he said, Go also you into the vineyard, and whatsoever may be just I will give you. And they went their way.

5 Again, having gone out about the sixth and ninth hour, he did likewise.

6 But about the eleventh [hour] having gone out, he found others standing, and says to them, Why stand you here all the day idle?

7 They say to him, Because no man has hired us. He says to them, Go also you into the vineyard [and whatsoever may be just you shall receive]

8 But when the evening was come, the lord of the vineyard says to his steward, Call the workmen and pay [them] their wages, beginning from the last even to the first.

9 And when they [who came to work] about the eleventh hour came, they received each a denarius.

10 And when the first came, they supposed that they would receive more, and they received also themselves each a denarius.

11 And on receiving it they murmured against the master of the house,

12 saying, These last have worked one hour, and you have made them equal to us, who have borne the burden of the day and the heat.

13 But he answering said to one of them, [my] friend, I do not wrong you. Did you not agree with me for a denarius?

14 Take what is yours and go. But it is my will to give to this last even as to you:

15 is it not lawful for me to do what I will in my own affairs? Is your eye evil because I am good?

16 Thus shall the last be first, and the first last; for many are called ones, but few chosen ones.

Lazarus' Illness

John 11:1 Now there was a certain [man] sick, Lazarus of Bethany, of the village of Mary and Martha her sister.

2 It was the Mary who anointed the Lord with ointment and wiped his feet with her hair, whose brother Lazarus was sick.

3 The sisters therefore sent to him, saying, Lord, behold, he whom you liked is sick.

4 But when Yehoshua heard it he said, This sickness is not unto death, but for the glory of the God, that the Son of the God may be glorified by it.

5 Now Yehoshua loved Martha, and her sister, and Lazarus.

6 When therefore he heard, He is sick, he remained two days then in the place where he was.

7 Then after this he says to his disciples, Let us go into Judea again.

8 The disciples say to him, Rabbi, [even but] now the Jews sought to stone you, and you go there again?

9 Yehoshua answered, Are there not twelve hours in the day? If any one walk in the day, he does not stumble, because he sees the light of this world;

10 but if any one walk in the night, he stumbles, because the light is not in him.

11 These things said he; and after this he says to them, Lazarus, our friend, is fallen asleep, but I go that I may awake him out of sleep.

12 The disciples therefore said to him, Lord, if he be fallen asleep, he will get well.

13 But Yehoshua spoke of his death, but they thought that he spoke of the rest of sleep.

14 Yehoshua therefore then said to them plainly, Lazarus has died.

15 And I rejoice on your account that I was not there, in order that you may believe. But let us go to him.

16 Thomas therefore, called Didymus, said to his fellow disciples, Let us also go, that we may die with him.

17 Yehoshua therefore [on] arriving found him to have been four days already in the tomb.

18 Now Bethany was near Jerusalem, about fifteen stadia off,

19 and many of the Jews came to Martha and Mary, that they might console them concerning their brother.

20 Martha then, when she heard Yehoshua is coming, went to meet him; but Mary sat in the house.

21 Martha therefore said to Yehoshua, Lord, if you had been here, my brother had not died;

22 but even now I know, that whatsoever you shall ask of the God, the God will give you.

23 Yehoshua says to her, Your brother shall rise again.

24 Martha says to him, I know that he will rise again in the resurrection in the last day.

25 Yehoshua said to her, I am the resurrection and the life: he that believes on me, though he has died, shall live;

26 and every one who lives and believes on me shall in no way die into the aeon [age]. Do you believe this?

27 She says to him, Yes, Lord; I believe that you are the Masiah, the Son of the God, who should come into the world.

28 And having said this, she went away and called her sister Mary secretly, saying, The teacher is come and calls you.

29 She, when she heard that rises up quickly and comes to him.

30 Now Yehoshua had not yet come into the village, but was in the place where Martha came to meet him.

31 The Jews therefore who were with her in the house and consoling her, seeing Mary that she rose up quickly and went out, followed her, saying, She

goes to the tomb, that she may weep there.

32 Mary therefore, when she came where Yehoshua was, seeing him, fell at his feet, saying to him, Lord, if you had been here, my brother would not have died.

33 Yehoshua therefore, when he saw her weeping, and the Jews who came with her weeping, was deeply moved in spirit, and was troubled,

34 and said, Where have you put him? They say to him, Lord, come and see.

35 Yehoshua wept.

36 The Jews therefore said, Behold how he liked him!

37 But some of them said, Could not this man, who opened the eyes of the blind man, have kept this man also from dying?

Lazarus Raised from the Dead

38 Yehoshua therefore, again deeply moved in himself, comes to the tomb. Now it was a cave, and a stone lay upon it.

39 Yehoshua says, Take away the stone. Martha, the sister of the dead, says to him, Lord, he stinks already, for he is four days [there]

40 Yehoshua says to her, Did I not say to you, that if you should believe, you should see the glory of the God?

41 They took therefore the stone away. And Yehoshua lifted up his eyes on high and said, Father, I thank you that you have heard me;

42 but I knew that you always hear me; but on account of the crowd who stand around I have said it that they may believe that you have sent me.

43 And having said this, he cried with a loud voice, Lazarus, come forth.

44 And the dead came forth, bound feet and hands with graveclothes, and his face was bound round with a handkerchief. Yehoshua says to them, Loosen him and let him go.

Sanhedrin Plots to Kill Masiah

45 Many therefore of the Jews who came to Mary and saw what he had done, believed on him;

46 but some of them went to the Pharisees and told them what Yehoshua had done.

47 The chief priests, therefore, and the Pharisees gathered a council, and said, What do we do? for this man does many signs.

48 If we leave him alone, all will believe on him, and the Romans will come and take away both our place and our nation.

49 But a certain one of them, Caiaphas, being high priest that year, said to them, You know nothing

50 nor consider that it is profitable for you that one man die for the people, and not that the whole nation perish.

51 But this he did not say of himself; but, being high priest that year, prophesied that Yehoshua was going to die for the nation;

52 and not for the nation only, but that he should also gather together into one the children of the God who were scattered abroad.

53 From that day therefore they took counsel that they might kill him.

Yehoshua withdraws to Ephraim

54 Yehoshua therefore walked no longer openly among the Jews, but went away from there into the country near the desert, to a city called Ephraim, and there he sojourned with the disciples.

On Divorce, When Two Become One they are One

Matt 19:3 And the Pharisees came to him testing him, and saying, Is it lawful for a man to put away his wife for every cause?

4 But he answering said [to them] Have you not read that he who made [them] from the beginning made them male and female,

5 and said, On account of this a man shall leave father and mother, and shall be united to his wife, and the two shall be one flesh?

6 so that they are no longer two, but one flesh. What therefore the God has joined together, let not man separate.

7 They say to him, Why then did Moses command to give a letter of divorce and to send [her] away?

8 He says to them, Moses, in view of your hardheartedness, allowed you to put away your wives; but from the beginning it was not thus.

9 But I say unto you, that whosoever shall put away his wife, not for fornication, and shall marry another, commits adultery; and he who marries one put away commits adultery.

10 His disciples say to him, If the case of the man be so with his wife, it is not good to marry.

11 And he said to them, All cannot receive this word, but those to whom it has been given;

12 for there are eunuchs which have been born thus from [their] mother's womb; and there are eunuchs who have been made eunuchs of men; and there are eunuchs who have made eunuchs of themselves for the sake of the kingdom of the heavens. He that is able to receive it let him receive it

Little Children

13 Then there were brought to him little children that he might lay his hands on them and pray; but the disciples rebuked them.

14 But Yehoshua said, Permit little children, and do not hinder them from coming to me; for the kingdom of the heavens is of such:

15 and having laid his hands upon them, he departed from there.

16 And lo, one coming up said to him, Teacher, what good thing shall I do that I may have aeonian life?

Buy Treasure in Heaven

17 And he said to him, Why ask me concerning goodness? One is good. But if you want to enter into life, keep the commandments.

18 He says to him, Which? And Yehoshua said, You shall not kill, You shall not commit adultery, You shall not steal, You shall not bear false witness,

19 honor your father and your mother, and You shall love your neighbor as yourself.

20 The young man says to him, All these have I kept; what lack I yet?

21 Yehoshua said to him, If you would be perfect, go, sell what you have and give to the poor, and you shall have treasure in heaven; and come, follow me.

22 But the young man, having heard the word, went away grieved, for he had large possessions.

Who Then can be Saved

23 And Yehoshua said to his disciples, Truly I say unto you, A rich man shall with difficulty enter into the kingdom of the heavens;

24 and again I say unto you, It is easier for a camel to enter a needle's eye than a rich man into the kingdom of the God.

25 And when the disciples heard it they were exceedingly astonished, saying, Who then can be saved?

26 But Yehoshua, looking on [them] said to them, With men this is impossible; but with God all things are possible.

Forsake All to Follow Masiah

27 Then Peter answering said to him, Behold, we have left all things and have followed you; what then shall happen to us?

28 And Yehoshua said to them, Truly I say unto you, That you who have followed me, in the regeneration when the Son of man shall sit down upon his throne of glory, you also shall sit on twelve thrones, judging the twelve tribes of Israel.

29 And every one who has left houses, or brethren, or sisters, or father, or mother, or wife, or children, or lands, for my name's sake, shall receive a hundredfold, and shall inherit aeonian life.

30 But many first shall be last, and last first.

Yehoshua Death Foretold Again

Mark 10:32 And they were in the way going up to Jerusalem, and Yehoshua was going on before them; and they were amazed, and were afraid as they followed. And taking the twelve again to him he began to tell them what was going to happen to him:

33 Behold, we go up to Jerusalem, and the Son of man shall be delivered up to the chief priests and to the scribes, and they shall condemn him to death, and shall deliver him up to the nations:

34 and they shall mock him, and shall scourge him, and shall spit upon him, and shall kill him; and after three days he shall rise again.

Luke 18:33 And when they have scourged him, they will kill him; and on the third day he will rise again.

34 And they understood nothing of these things. And this word was hidden from them, and they did not know what was said.

James and John Wish to Sit on Masiah's Right and Left Side

Mark 10:35 And there come to him James and John, the sons of Zebedee, saying [to him] Teacher, we wish that whatsoever we may ask you, you would do it for us. [Their mother came with them and asked the question for them (Mat 20:20-21).]

36 And he said to them, What do you wish that I should do for you?

37 And they said to him, Give to us that we may sit, one on your right hand, and one on your left hand, in your glory.

38 And Yehoshua said to them, You do not know what you ask. Are you able to drink the cup which I drink, or be baptized with the baptism that I am baptized with?

39 And they said to him, We are able. And Yehoshua said to them, The cup that I drink you will drink and with the baptism that I am baptized with you will be baptized,

40 but to sit on my right hand or on my left is not mine to give, but for those for whom it is prepared.

41 And the ten having heard [of it] began to be indignant about James and John.

42 But Yehoshua having called them to him, says to them, You know that those who are esteemed to rule over the nations exercise lordship over them; and their great men exercise authority over them;

43 but it is not thus among you; but whosoever would be great among you, shall be your minister;

44 and whosoever would be first of you shall be servant of all.

45 For also the Son of man did not come to be ministered to, but to minister, and give his soul a ransom for many.

Zacchaeus Receives Yehoshua

Luke 19:1 And he entered and passed through Jericho.

2 And behold, [there was] a man by name called Zacchaeus, and he was chief tax-gatherer, and he was rich.

3 And he sought to see Yehoshua who he was: and he could not for the crowd, because he was little in stature.

4 And running on before, he got up into a sycamore that he might see him, for he was going to pass that [way]

5 And when he came up to the place, Yehoshua looked up and saw him, and said to him, Zacchaeus, make haste and come down, for today I must remain in your house.

6 And he made haste and came down, and received him with joy.

7 And all murmured when they saw it saying, He has turned in to lodge with a sinful man.

8 But Zacchaeus stood and said to the Lord, Behold, Lord, half of my goods I give to the poor, and if I have taken anything from any man by false accusation, I return him fourfold.

9 And Yehoshua said to him, Today salvation is come to this house, inasmuch as he also is a son of Abraham;

10 for the Son of man has come to seek and to save that which is lost.

Blind Beggar Healed

Mark 10:46 And they come to Jericho, and as he was going out from Jericho, and his disciples and a large crowd, the son of Timaeus, Bartimaeus, the blind [man] sat by the wayside begging.

47 And having heard that it was Yehoshua the Nazarene, he began to cry out and to say, O Son of David, Yehoshua, have mercy on me.

48 And many rebuked him, that he might be silent; but he cried so much the more, Son of David, have mercy on me.

49 And Yehoshua, standing still, desired him to be called. And they call the blind [man] saying to him, Be of good courage, rise up, he calls you.

50 And, throwing away his garment, he started up and came to Yehoshua.

51 And Yehoshua answering says to him, What do you wish that I shall do to you? And the blind [man] said to him, Rabboni, that I may see.

52 And Yehoshua said to him, Go, your faith has healed you. And he saw immediately, and followed him in the way.

Parable of Ten Minas (Pounds)

Luke 19:11 But as they were listening to these things, he added and spoke a parable, because he was near to Jerusalem and they thought that the kingdom of the God was about to be immediately manifested.

12 He said therefore, A certain nobleman went to a distant country to receive for himself a kingdom and return.

13 And having called his own ten servants, he gave to them ten minas, and said to them, Trade while I am coming.

14 But his citizens hated him, and sent an embassy after him, saying, We do not want that this [nobleman] to reign over us.

15 And it came to pass on his arrival back again, having received the kingdom, that he desired these servants to whom he gave the money to be called to him, in order that he might know what every one had gained by trading.

16 And the first came up, saying, [my] Lord, your mina has produced ten minas.

17 And he said to him, Well [done] you good servant; because you have been faithful in that which is least, be you in authority over ten cities.

18 And the second came, saying, [my] Lord, your mina has made five minas.

19 And he said also to this one, And you, be over five cities.

20 And another came, saying, [my] Lord, lo, [there is] your mina, which I have kept laid up in a towel.

21 For I feared you because you are a harsh man: you take up what you have not laid down, and you reap what you have not sowed.

22 He says to him, Out of your mouth will I judge you, wicked servant: you knew that I am a harsh man, taking up what I have not laid down and reaping what I have not sowed.

23 And why did you not give my money to the bank; and I should have received it, at my coming, with interest?

24 And he said to those that stood by, Take from him the mina and give it to him who has the ten minas.

25 And they said to him, Lord, he has ten minas.

26 For I say unto you, that to every one that has shall be given; but from him that has not, that even which he has shall be taken from him.

27 Moreover mine enemies, who would not [have] me to reign over them, bring them here and slay [them] before me.

Yehoshua Continues on Toward Jerusalem

28 And having said these things, he went on before, going up to Jerusalem.

Arrest of Yehoshua Planned for Passover

John 11:55 But the Passover of the Jews was near, and many went up to Jerusalem out of the country before the Passover, that they might purify themselves.

56 They sought therefore Yehoshua, and said among themselves, standing in the temple, What do you think? that he will not come to the feast?

57 Now the chief priests and the Pharisees had given commandment that if any one knew where he was, he should make it known, that they might take him.

Last Week of Yehoshua's Ministry on Earth

Evening of the 9th of Nisan[20]

Mary Anoints Yehoshua's Feet

John 12:1 Yehoshua therefore, six days before the Passover, came to Bethany, where was the dead [man] Lazarus, whom Yehoshua raised from among the dead.

2 There therefore they made him a supper, and Martha served, but Lazarus was one of those at table with him.

3 Mary therefore, having taken a pound of ointment of pure nard of great price, anointed the feet of Yehoshua, and wiped his feet with her hair, and the house was filled with the odor of the ointment.

4 One of his disciples therefore, Judas [son] of Simon, Iscariote, who was about to deliver him up, says,

5 Why was this ointment not sold for three hundred denarii and given to the poor?

6 But he said this, not that he cared for the poor, but because he was a thief and had the bag, and carried what was put into it

7 Yehoshua therefore said, Permit her to keep this for the day of my preparation for burial;

8 for you have the poor always with you, but me you do not have always.

---

[20] The month of Nisan was the Jews 1st month of their holy calendar; the Passover was killed on the 14th of Nisan; the 15th & 21st of Nisan were holy Sabbaths. See New Mind Papers (NM16) for details.

Night of the 10th of Nisan

Plot also to Kill Yehoshua and Lazarus

Luke 22:3 And Satan entered into Judas, who was surnamed Iscariote, being of the number of the twelve.

4 And he went away and spoke with the chief priests and captains as to how he should deliver him up to them.

5 And they were rejoiced, and agreed to give him money. [30 pieces of silver, Matt 26:15-16; Zech 11:12]

6 And he came to an agreement to do it, and sought an opportunity to deliver him up to them away from the crowd.

John 12:9 A great crowd therefore of the Jews knew that he was there; and they came, not because of Yehoshua only, but also that they might see Lazarus whom he raised from among the dead.

10 But the chief priests took counsel that they might kill Lazarus also,

11 because many of the Jews went away on his account and believed on Yehoshua.

Daylight of the 10th Nisan

Jerusalem Crowd Greets Yehoshua with Palms and, "Blessed is the King of Israel"

12 On the next day a great crowd who came to the feast, having heard that Yehoshua is coming into Jerusalem,

13 took branches of palms and went out to meet him, and cried, Hosanna, blessed [is] he that comes in the name of the Lord, the King of Israel.

Yehoshua Sends for Colt

Luke 19:29 And it came to pass as he drew near to Bethphage and Bethany at the mountain called [the mount] of Olives, he sent two of his disciples,

30 saying, Go into the village over against [you] in which you will find, on entering it, a colt tied up, on which no [child] of man ever sat at any time: loose it and lead it [here]

31 And if any one ask you, Why do you loose it thus shall you say to him, Because the Lord has need of it.

32 And they that were sent, having gone their way, found as he had said to them.

33 And as they were loosing the colt, its masters said to them, Why loose you the colt?

34 And they said, Because the Lord has need of it.

Matt 21:4 But all this came to pass, that that might be fulfilled which was spoken through the prophet, saying,

5 Say to the daughter of Zion, Behold your King comes to you, meek, and mounted upon an donkey, and upon a colt the foal of an donkey.

Luke 19:35 And they led it to Yehoshua; and having cast their own garments on the colt, they put Yehoshua on it

36 And as he went, they scattered their clothes in the way.

Yehoshua Comes to Jerusalem

37 And as he drew near, already at the descent of the mount of Olives, all the multitude of the disciples began, rejoicing, to praise the God with a loud voice for all the works of power which they had seen,

38 saying, Blessed the King that comes in the name of the Lord: peace in heaven, and glory in the highest.

39 And some of the Pharisees from the crowd said to him, Teacher, rebuke your disciples.

40 And he answering said to them, I say unto you, If these shall be silent, the stones will cry out.

Yehoshua Foretells of the Destruction of Jerusalem

41 And as he drew near, seeing the city, he wept over it,

42 saying, If you had known, even you, even at least in this your day, the things that are for your peace: but now they are hid from your eyes;

43 for days shall come upon you, that your enemies shall make a embankment about you, and shall close you around, and keep you in on every side,

44 and shall lay you even with the ground, and your children in you; and shall not leave in you a stone upon a stone: because you knew not the season of your visitation.

Yehoshua Enters Jerusalem

Matt 21:10 And as he entered into Jerusalem, the whole city was moved, saying, Who is this?

11 And the crowds said, This is Yehoshua the prophet who is from Nazareth of Galilee.

Evening of the 10th of Nisan

Mark 11:11 And he entered into Jerusalem and into the temple; and having looked round on all things, the hour being already late, he went out to Bethany with the twelve.

Daylight of the 11th of Nisan

Fig Tree

12 And on the next day [after spending the night in Bethany, v. 11], when they were gone out of Bethany, he hungered.

13 And seeing from afar off a fig-tree which had leaves, he came, if perhaps he might find something on it. And having come up to it he found nothing but leaves, for it was not the time of figs.

14 And answering he said to it, Let no one eat fruit of you any more into the aeon. And his disciples heard it

Enters Temple and Cleanses It

15 And they come to Jerusalem, and entering into the temple, he began to cast out those who sold and who bought in the temple, and he overthrew the tables of the moneychangers and the seats of the dove-sellers,

16 and permitted not that any one should carry any package through the temple.

17 And he taught saying to them, Is it not written, My house shall be called a house of prayer for all the nations? but you have made it a den of robbers.

Plot to Kill Yehoshua Delayed

18 And the chief priests and the scribes heard it and they sought how they might destroy him; for they feared him, because all the crowd were astonished at his doctrine.

Luke 19:47 And he was teaching day by day in the temple: and the chief priests and the scribes and the chief of the people sought to destroy him,

48 and did not find what they could do, for all the people hung on him to hear.

Children Praise Yehoshua

Matt 21:14 And blind and lame came to him in the temple, and he healed them.

15 And when the chief priests and the scribes saw the wonders which he worked, and the children crying in the temple and saying, Hosanna to the Son of David, they were indignant,

16 and said to him, Do you hear what these say? And Yehoshua says to them, Yes; have you never read, Out of the mouth of babes and sucklings you have perfected praise?

Yehoshua Death's Purpose: To Draw All

John 12:20 And there were certain Greeks among those who came up that they might worship in the feast;

21 these therefore came to Philip, who was of Bethsaida of Galilee, and they asked him saying, Sir, we desire to see Yehoshua.

22 Philip comes and tells Andrew, [and again] Andrew comes and Philip, and they tell Yehoshua.

23 But Yehoshua answered them saying, The hour is come that the Son of man should be glorified.

24 Truly, truly, I say unto you, Except the grain of wheat falling into the ground die, it abides alone; but if it die, it bears much fruit. [see verse 32 = all]

25 He that likes his soul shall lose it, and he that hates his soul in this world shall keep it to aeonian life.

26 If any one serve me, let him follow me; and where I am, there also shall be my servant. [and] if any one serve me, him shall the Father honor.

Time for the Prince of the World to be Driven Out

27 Now is my soul troubled, and what shall I say? Father, save me from this hour. But on account of this have I come to this hour.

28 Father, glorify your name. There came therefore a voice out of heaven, I both have glorified and will glorify it again.

29 The crowd therefore, which stood [there] and heard it said that it had thundered. Others said, An angel has spoken to him.

30 Yehoshua answered and said, Not on my account has this voice come, but on yours.

31 Now is the judgment of this world; now shall the prince of this world be cast out:

32 and I, if I be lifted up out of the earth, will draw all to me.

33 But this he said signifying by what death he was about to die.

Walk in the Light

34 The crowd answered him, We have heard out of the law that the Masiah abides into the aeon; and how can you say that the Son of man must be lifted up? Who is this, the Son of man?

35 Yehoshua therefore said to them, Yet a little while is the light among you. Walk while you have the light, that darkness may not overtake you. And he who walks in the darkness does not know where he goes.

36 While you have the light, believe in the light, that you may become sons of light. Yehoshua said these things, and going away hid himself from them.

Night of the 12th of Nisan

After Day in Jerusalem, Yehoshua went back to Bethany

Mark 11:19 And when it was evening he went forth outside the city.

Daylight of the 12th of Nisan

Fig Tree Lesson: Faith

Mark 11:20 And passing by early in the morning they saw the fig-tree dried up from the roots.

21 And Peter, remembering [what Yehoshua had said] says to him, Rabbi, see, the fig-tree which you cursed is dried up.

22 And Yehoshua answering says to them, Have faith in God.

23 Truly I say to you, that whosoever shall say to this mountain, Be you taken away and cast into the sea, and shall not doubt in his heart, but believe that what he says takes place, whatever he shall say shall come to pass for him.

24 For this reason I say to you, All things whatsoever you pray for and ask, believe that you receive it, and it shall come to pass for you.

25 And when you stand praying, forgive if you have anything against any one, that your Father also who is in the heavens may forgive you your offences.

26 But if you do not forgive, neither will your Father who is in the heavens forgive your offences.

Chief Priests Question Yehoshua's Authority

27 And they come again to Jerusalem. And as he walked about in the temple, the chief priests and the scribes and the elders come to him,

28 and they say to him, By what authority do you do these things? and who gave you this authority, that you should do these things?

29 And Yehoshua answering said to them, I also will ask you one thing, and answer me, and I will tell you by what authority I do these things:

30 The baptism of John, was it of heaven, or of men? answer me.

31 And they reasoned with themselves, saying, If we should say, Of heaven, he will say, Why [then] have you not believed him?

32 but should we say, Of men – they feared the people; for all held of John that he was truly a prophet.

33 And they answering say to Yehoshua, We do not know. And Yehoshua [answering] says to them, Neither do I tell you by what authority I do these things.

Parable of two Sons

Matt 21:28 But what do you think? A man had two children, and coming to the first he said, Child, go today, work in [my] vineyard.

29 And he answering said, I will not; but afterwards repenting he went.

30 And coming to the second he said likewise; and he answering said, I [go] sir, and went not.

31 Which of the two did the will of the father? They say [to him] The first. Yehoshua says to them, Truly I say unto you that the tax-gatherers and the harlots go into the kingdom of the God before you.

32 For John came to you in the way of righteousness, and you believed him not; but the tax-gatherers and the harlots believed him; but you when you saw it repented not yourselves afterwards to believe him.

Parable of Tenants who Kills the Son of the Owner

Mark 12:1 And he began to say to them in parables, A man planted a vineyard, and made a fence round it and dug a wine-vat, and built a tower, and let it out to husbandmen, and left the country.

2 And he sent a servant to the husbandmen at the season, that he might receive from the husbandmen of the fruit of the vineyard.

3 But they took him, and beat him, and sent him away empty.

4 And again he sent to them another servant; and [at] him they [threw stones, and] struck him on the head, and sent him away with insult.

5 And [again] he sent another, and him they killed; and many others, beating some and killing some.

6 Having yet therefore one beloved son, he sent also him to them the last, saying, They will have respect for my son.

7 But those husbandmen said to one another, This is the heir: come, let us kill him and the inheritance will be ours.

8 And they took him and killed him, and cast him forth out of the vineyard.

9 What therefore shall the lord of the vineyard do? He will come and destroy the husbandmen, and will give the vineyard to others.

Luke 20:16 He will come and destroy those husbandmen, and will give the vineyard to others. And when they heard it they said, May it never be!

Parable of the Rejected Stone

Matt 21:42 Yehoshua says to them, Have you never read in the scriptures, The stone which they that builded rejected, this has become the corner-stone: this is of the Lord, and it is wonderful in our eyes?

43 Therefore I say to you, that the kingdom of the God shall be taken from you and shall be given to a nation producing the fruits of it.

44 And he that falls on this stone[21] shall be broken, but on whomsoever it shall fall, it shall grind him to powder.

Jewish Leaders Look for a way to Arrest Yehoshua

45 And the chief priests and the Pharisees, having heard his parables, knew that he spoke about them.

46 And seeking to lay hold of him, they were afraid of the crowds, because they believed him to be a prophet.

Parable of Wedding Banquet

Matt 22:1 And Yehoshua answering spoke to them again in parables, saying,

2 The kingdom of the heavens has become like a king who made a wedding feast for his son,

3 and sent his servants to call the persons invited to the wedding feast, and they would not come.

4 Again he sent other servants, saying, Say to the persons invited, Behold, I have prepared my dinner; my oxen and my fatted beasts are killed, and all things ready; come to the wedding feast.

5 But they made light of it, and went, one to his own land, and another to his commerce.

6 And the rest, laying hold of his servants, ill-treated and slew [them]

7 And [when] the king [heard of it he] was wrathful, and having sent his forces, destroyed those murderers and burned their city.

8 Then he says to his servants, The wedding feast is ready, but those invited were not worthy;

9 go therefore into the thoroughfares of the highways, and as many as you shall find invite to the wedding feast.

---

[21] Yehoshua is that stone v. 42

10 And those servants went out into the highways, and brought together all as many as they found, both evil and good; and the wedding feast was furnished with guests.

11 And the king, having gone in to see the guests, beheld there a man not clothed with a wedding garment.

12 And he says to him, [my] friend, how camest you in here not having on a wedding garment? But he was speechless.

13 Then said the king to the servants, Bind him feet and hands, and take him away, and cast him out into the outer darkness: there shall be the weeping and the gnashing of teeth.

14 For many are called ones, but few chosen ones.

Pharisees Ask About Taxes

15 Then went the Pharisees and held a council how they might ensnare him in speaking.

16 And they send out to him their disciples with the Herodians, saying, Teacher, we know that you are true and teach the way of the God in truth, and care not for any one, for you regard not men's person;

17 tell us therefore what you think: Is it lawful to give tribute to Caesar, or not?

18 But Yehoshua, knowing their wickedness, said, Why do you test me, hypocrites?

19 Show me the money of the tribute. And they presented to him a denarius.

20 And he says to them, Whose [is] this image and superscription?

21 They say to him, Caesar's. Then he says to them, Pay then what is Caesar's to Caesar, and what is God's to the God.

Sadducess ask about Resurrection

22 And when they heard him, they wondered, and left him, and went away.

23 On that day came to him Sadducees, who say there is no resurrection; and they asked of him,

24 saying, Teacher, Moses said, If any one die, not having children, his brother shall marry his wife and shall raise up seed to his brother.

25 Now there were with us seven brethren; and the first having married died, and not having seed, left his wife to his brother.

26 In like manner also the second and the third, unto the seven.

27 And last of all the woman also died.

28 In the resurrection therefore of which of the seven shall she be wife, for all had her?

29 And Yehoshua answering said to them, You err, not knowing the scriptures nor the power of the God.

30 For in the resurrection they neither marry nor are given in marriage, but are as angels of the God in heaven.

31 But concerning the resurrection of the dead, have you not read what was spoken to you by the God, saying,

32 I am God of Abraham, and the God of Isaac, and the God of Jacob? the God is not God of the dead, but of the living.

33 And when the crowds heard it they were astonished at his doctrine.

Greatest Commandment

Mark 12:28 And one of the scribes who had come up, and had heard them reasoning together, perceiving that he had answered them well, asked of him, Which is the first commandment of all?

29 And Yehoshua answered him, the first commandment of all [is] Hear, Israel: the Lord our God is one Lord [see Deu 6:4: "Lord = YHWH];

30 and you shall love the Lord your God with all your heart, and with all your soul, and with all your understanding,

and with all your strength. This is the first commandment.

31 And a second like it [is] this: You shall love your neighbor as yourself. There is not another commandment greater than these.

32 And the scribe said to him, Right, teacher; you have spoken according to the truth. For he is one, and there is none other besides him;

33 and to love him with all the heart, and with all the intelligence, and with all the soul, and with all the strength, and to love one's neighbor as one's self, is more than all the burnt-offerings and sacrifices.

34 And Yehoshua, seeing that he had answered intelligently, said to him, You are not far from the kingdom of the God. And no one dared question him any more.

Whose Son is the Messiah?

Matt 22:41 And the Pharisees being gathered together, Yehoshua asked of them,

42 saying, What do you think concerning the Masiah? whose son is he? They say to him, David's.

43 He says to them, How then does David in Spirit call him Lord, saying,

44 The Lord said to my Lord, Sit on my right hand until I put your enemies under your feet?

45 If therefore David call him Lord, how is he his son?

46 And no one was able to answer him a word, nor did any one dare from that day to question him any more.

Mark 12:37 David himself [therefore] calls him Lord, and how is he his son? And the mass of the people heard him gladly.

The Followers of Yehoshua's have One Teacher

Matt 23:1 Then Yehoshua spoke to the crowds and to his disciples,

2 saying, The scribes and the Pharisees have set themselves down in Moses' seat:

3 all things therefore, whatever he[22] [Moses] may tell you, do and keep. But do not after their [Pharisees] works, for they say and do not,

4 but bind burdens heavy and hard to bear, and lay them on the shoulders of men, but will not move them with their finger.

5 And all their works they do to be seen of men: for they make broad their phylacteries [boxes containing verses] and enlarge the borders [of their garments]

6 and like the chief place in feasts and the first seats in the synagogues,

7 and salutations in the market-places, and to be called of men, Rabbi, Rabbi.

8 But you, be not you called Rabbi; for one is your instructor, and all you are brethren.

9 And call not [any one] your father upon the earth; for one is your Father, he who is in the heavens.

10 Neither be called instructors, for one is your instructor, the Masiah.

11 But the greatest of you shall be your servant.

12 And whoever shall exalt himself shall be humbled, and whoever shall humble himself shall be exalted.

Old Teachers of the Law were Hypocrites

13 But woe unto you, scribes and Pharisees, hypocrites, for you shut up

---

[22]"He" as per Hebrew texts found by Nehemia Gordon

the kingdom of the heavens before men; for you do not enter, nor do you permit those that are entering to go in.

[14 Woe to you, scribes and Pharisees, hypocrites! For you devour widows' houses, and for a pretense make long prayer: therefore you shall receive the greater judgment.]

15 Woe to you, scribes and Pharisees, hypocrites, for you compass the sea and the dry [land] to make one proselyte, and when he is become [such] you make him twofold more the son of hell [Gehenna] than yourselves.

Swearing

16 Woe to you, blind guides, who say, Whosoever shall swear by the temple, it is nothing; but whosoever shall swear by the gold of the temple, he is a debtor.

17 Fools and blind, for which is greater, the gold, or the temple which sanctifies the gold?

18 And, Whosoever shall swear by the altar, it is nothing; but whosoever shall swear by the gift that is upon it is a debtor.

19 [Fools and] blind ones, for which is greater, the gift, or the altar which sanctifies the gift?

20 He therefore that swears by the altar swears by it and by all things that are upon it.

21 And he that swears by the temple swears by it and by him that dwells in it.

22 And he that swears by heaven swears by the throne of the God and by him that sits upon it.

Legalism versus what is Important

23 Woe to you, scribes and Pharisees, hypocrites, for you pay tithes of mint and anise and cummin, and you have left aside the weightier matters of the law, judgment and mercy and faith: these you ought to have done and not have left those aside.

24 Blind guides, who strain out the gnat, but drink down the camel.

Hypocrisy of Appearance

25 Woe to you, scribes and Pharisees, hypocrites, for you make clean the outside of the cup and of the dish, but within they are full of greed and intemperance.

26 Blind Pharisee, make clean first the inside of the cup and of the dish, that their outside also may become clean.

27 Woe to you, scribes and Pharisees, hypocrites, for you are like whitened tombs, which appear beautiful outwardly, but within are full of dead men's bones and all uncleanness.

28 Thus also you, outwardly you appear righteous to men, but within are full of hypocrisy and lawlessness.

Persecution of Prophets

29 Woe to you, scribes and Pharisees, hypocrites, for you build the tombs of the prophets and adorn the tombs of the just,

30 and you say, If we had been in the days of our fathers we would not have been partakers with them in the blood of the prophets.

31 So that you bear witness of yourselves that you are sons of those who slew the prophets:

32 and you, fill you up the measure of your fathers.

33 Serpents, offspring of vipers, how should you escape the judgment of hell [Gehenna]?

34 Therefore, behold, I send unto you prophets, and wise men, and scribes; and [some] of them you will kill and crucify, and [some] of them you will scourge in your synagogues, and will persecute from city to city;

35 so that all righteous blood shed upon the earth should come upon you, from the blood of righteous Abel to the blood

of Zacharias son of Barachias, whom you slew between the temple and the altar.

36 Truly I say unto you, All these things shall come upon this generation.

O Jerusalem, O Jerusalem

37 Jerusalem, Jerusalem, [the city] that kills the prophets and stones those that are sent unto her, how often would I have gathered your children as a hen gathers her chickens under her wings, and you would not!

38 Behold, your house is left unto you desolate;

39 for I say unto you, You shall in no way see me henceforth until you say, Blessed [be] he that comes in the name of the Lord.

Poor Widow's Gift

Mark 12:41 And Yehoshua, having sat down opposite the treasury, saw how the crowd was casting money into the treasury; and many rich cast in much.

42 And a poor widow came and cast in two bits [lepta] which is a quarter [quadrans]

43 And having called his disciples to him, he said to them, Truly I say unto you, This poor widow has cast in more than all who have cast into the treasury:

44 for all have cast in of that which they had in abundance, but she of her destitution has cast in all that she had, the whole of her living.

End Time Events

Temple to be Destroyed

Mark 13:1 And as he was going out of the temple, one of his disciples says to him, Teacher, see what stones and what buildings!

2 And Yehoshua answering said to him, See you these great buildings? not a stone shall be left upon a stone, which shall not be thrown down.

3 And as he sat on the mount of Olives opposite the temple, Peter and James and John and Andrew asked him privately,

4 Tell us, when shall these things be, and what is the sign when all these things are going to be fulfilled?

Matt 24:3 And as he was sitting upon the mount of Olives the disciples came to him privately, saying, Tell us, when shall these things be, and what is the sign of your coming and the completion of the age [aeon].

Note: We will start in the next section to use three column tables to portray the sayings of Yehoshua that pertain to the signs of the end time. This should make it easier for you to compare the somewhat different renditions of these events.

Masiah's Signs of the End -Time

Mark 13:3 And as he sat on the mount of Olives opposite the temple, Peter and James and John and Andrew asked him privately, 4 **Tell us, when shall these things be, and what is the sign when all these things are going to be fulfilled?** 5 And Yehoshua answering them began to say, Take heed lest any one mislead you. 6 For many shall come in my name, saying, It is I, and shall mislead many. 7 But when you shall hear of wars and rumours of wars, be not disturbed, for [this] must happen, **but the end is not yet.**	Matt 24:3 And as he was sitting upon the mount of Olives the disciples came to him privately, saying, Tell us, when shall these things be, and **what is the sign of your coming and the completion of the age [aeon]** 4 And Yehoshua answering said to them, See that no one mislead you. 5 For many shall come in my name, saying, I am the Masiah, and they shall mislead many. 6 But you will hear of wars and rumors of wars. See that you be not disturbed; for all [these things] must take place, **but it is not yet the end.**	Luke 21:7 And they asked him saying, Teacher, **when then shall these things be; and what [is] the sign when these things are going to take place?** 8 And he said, See that you be not led astray, for many shall come in my name, saying, I am he, and the time is drawn near: go you not [therefore] after them. 9 And when you shall hear of wars and revolutions, be not terrified, for these things must first take place, **but the end is not immediately.**
The Last Wars, Great Earthquakes, Famine and Pestilence		
Mark 13:8 For **nation shall rise up against nation**, and kingdom against kingdom; and there shall be earthquakes in [different] places, and there shall be famines and troubles: these things [are the] **beginnings of throes.**	Matt 24:7 For **nation shall rise up against nation,** and kingdom against kingdom; and there shall be famines and pestilences, and earthquakes in diverse places. 8 But all these [are the] **beginning of throes.**	Luke 21:10 Then he said to them, **Nation shall rise up against nation**, and kingdom against kingdom; 11 there shall be both great earthquakes in different places, and famine and pestilence; and there shall be fearful sights and great signs from heaven.

Church Persecution

Before the 3 1/2 years, *during* the 3 1/2 years, and *at the End* (Rev 3:14-22; Dan 11:33-35; 12:10; Mal 3:3)

Mark 13:9 But you, take heed to yourselves, for **they shall deliver you [disciples] up** to sanhedrims and to synagogues: you shall be beaten and brought before rulers and kings for my sake, for a testimony to them; 10 and the gospel must first be preached to all the nations. 11 But when they shall lead you away to deliver you up, be not concerned beforehand as to what you shall say, [nor prepare your discourse] but whatsoever shall be given you in that hour, that speak; for you are not the speakers, but the Holy Spirit. 12 But brother shall deliver up brother to death, and father child; and children shall rise up against parents, and cause them to be put to death. 13 And you will be hated of all on account of my name; but he that has endured to the end, he shall be saved.	Matt 24:9 Then shall **they deliver you** [disciples] **up to tribulation**, and shall kill you; and you will be hated of all the nations for my name's sake. 10 And then will many be offended, and will deliver one another up, and hate one another; 11 and **many false prophets shall arise and shall mislead many**; 12 and because **lawlessness shall prevail, the love of the most shall grow cold;** 13 but he that has endured to the end, he shall be saved. 14 And these **good news of the kingdom shall be preached in the whole habitable earth, for a witness to all the nations, and then shall come the end.**	DBY Luke 21:12 But before all these things **they shall lay their hands upon you [disciples] and persecute you**, delivering [you] up to synagogues and prisons, bringing [you] before kings and governors on account of my name; 13 but it shall turn out to you for a testimony. 14 Settle therefore in your hearts not to meditate beforehand [your] defense, 15 for I will give you a mouth and wisdom which all your opposers shall not be able to reply to or resist. 16 But ye will be delivered up even by parents and brethren and relations and friends, and they shall put to death [some] from among you, 17 and ye will be hated of all for my name's sake. 18 And a hair of your head shall in no wise perish. 19 By your patient endurance gain your souls.

Great Tribulation

Tribulation before the end but the end is the greatest of all tribulations–**the Great Tribulation**
Abomination of Desolation / Beast – the last 1/2 week of years of the 70 weeks
of Dan 9:24-27
(Dan 9:27; 11:31; Rev 13:5; Dan 7:25; 12:7)

Mark 13:14 But when you shall see the **abomination of desolation standing where it should not**, he that reads let him consider it then let those in Judea flee to the mountains;	Matt 24:15 When therefore you shall see the **abomination of desolation**, which is spoken of through Daniel the prophet, **standing in [what is a] holy place**, he that reads let him understand,	Luke 21:20 But when ye see **Jerusalem encompassed with armies**, then know that its desolation is drawn nigh.
15 and him that is upon the housetop not come down into the house, nor enter [into it] to take away anything out of his house;	16 then let those who are in Judea flee to the mountains;	21 Then let those who are in Judaea flee to the mountains, and those who are in the midst of it depart out, and those who are in the country not enter into it; 22 for these are days of avenging, that all the things that are written may be accomplished. 23 But woe to them that are with child and to them who give suck in those days, for **there shall be great distress upon the land and wrath upon this people**. 24 And they shall fall by the edge of the sword, and be led captive into all the nations; and **Jerusalem shall be trodden down of the nations until the times of the nations be fulfilled**.
16 and him that is in the field not return back to take his garment.	17 let not him that is on the house come down to take the things out of his house;	
17 But woe to those that are with child and to those that give suck in those days!	18 and let not him that is in the field turn back to take his garment.	
18 And pray that it may not be in winter time;	19 But woe to those that are with child, and those that give suck in those days.	
19 for those days **shall be distress** such as there has not been the like since the beginning of creation which the God created, until now, and never shall be;	20 But pray that your flight may not be in winter time nor on Sabbath:	
20 and if the Lord had not cut off those days, **no flesh should have been saved; but on account of the elect whom he has chosen, he has cut off those days**.	21 for **then shall there be great tribulation**, such as has not been from the beginning of the world until now, nor ever shall be;	[DBY Ezekiel 38:16 And thou shalt come up against my people Israel as a cloud to cover the land– it shall be at the end of days– and I will bring thee against my land, that the nations may know me, when I shall be hallowed in thee, O Gog, before their eyes. 17 Thus saith the Lord Jehovah: Are thou not he of whom I have spoken in old time through my servants the prophets of Israel, who prophesied in those days, for [many] years, that I would bring thee against them? 18 And it shall come to pass in that day, in the day when Gog shall come against the land of Israel, saith the Lord Jehovah, that my fury shall come up in my face.... Revelation 16:14 for they are the spirits of demons,
21 And then if any one say to you, Lo, here [is] the Masiah, or Lo, there, believe it not.	22 and if those days had not been cut off, **no flesh had been saved; but on account of the elect those days shall be cut off**.	
22 For false Masiahs and false prophets will arise, and give signs and wonders to deceive, if possible, even the elect.	23 Then if any one say to you, Behold, here is the Masiah, or here, believe it not.	
23 But do you take heed:	24 For there shall arise false Masiahs, and false prophets, and shall give great signs and wonders,	

behold, I have told you all things beforehand.	so as to mislead, if possible, even the elect. 25 Behold, I have told you beforehand. 26 If therefore they say to you, Behold, he is in the desert, go not forth; behold, [he is] in the inner chambers, do not believe it	doing signs; which go out to the kings of the whole habitable world to gather them together to the war of that great day of God the Almighty.... 16 And he gathered them together to the place called in Hebrew, Armagedon. Revelation 19:19 And I saw the beast and the kings of the earth and their armies gathered together to make war against him that sat upon the horse, and against his army. Revelation 20:9 And they went up on the breadth of the earth, and surrounded the camp of the saints and the beloved city: and fire came down [from God] out of the heaven and devoured them.]

Immediately *After* the Great Tribulation
Comes the Salvation

Mark 13:24 But in those days, **after that distress**, the sun shall be darkened and the moon shall not give its light; 25 and the stars of heaven shall be falling down, and the powers which are in the heavens shall be shaken; 26 and then shall they see the Son of man coming in clouds with great power and glory; 27 and then shall he **send his angels** and shall gather together his elect from the four winds, from end of earth to end of heaven.	Matt 24:29 But **immediately after the tribulation of those days** the sun shall be darkened, and the moon not give her light, and the stars shall fall from heaven, and the powers of the heavens shall be shaken. 30 And then shall appear the sign of the Son of man in heaven; and then shall all the tribes of the land lament, and they shall see the Son of man coming on the clouds of heaven with power and great glory. 31 And he shall **send his angels with a great sound of trumpet**, and they shall gather together his elect from the four winds, from [the one] extremity of the heavens to [the other] extremity of them.	Luke 21:25 And there shall be signs in sun and moon and stars, and upon the earth distress of nations in perplexity [at] the roar of the sea and rolling waves, 26 men ready to die through fear and expectation of what is coming on the habitable earth, for the powers of the heavens shall be shaken. 27 And then shall they see the Son of man coming in a cloud with power and great glory. 28 But when these things begin to come to pass, look up and lift up your heads, because your redemption draws near.
Mark 13:28 But learn the parable from the **fig-tree**: when its branch already becomes tender and puts	Matt 24:32 But learn the parable from the **fig-tree**: When already its branch becomes tender and	Luke 21:29 And he spoke a parable to them: Behold the **fig-tree** and all the trees;

forth the leaves, you know that the summer is near.	produces leaves, you know that the summer is near.	30 when they already sprout, you know of your own selves, [on] looking [at them] that already the summer is near.
29 Thus also you, when you see these things happening, know that it is near, at the doors.	33 Thus also you, when you see all these things, know that it is near, at the doors.	31 So also you, when you see these things take place, know that the kingdom of the God is near.
30 Truly I say unto you, This generation shall in no way pass away, till all these things take place.	34 Truly I say to you, This generation will not have passed away until all these things shall have taken place.	32 Truly I say unto you, that this generation shall in no way pass away until all come to pass.
31 The heaven and the earth shall pass away, but my words shall in no way pass away.	35 The heaven and the earth shall pass away, but my words shall in no way pass away.	33 The heaven and the earth shall pass away, but my words shall in no way pass away.
	Matt 24:27 For as the **lightning** goes forth from the east and shines to the west, so shall be the coming of the Son of man.	Luke 17:24 For as the **lightning** shines which lightens from [one end] under heaven to [the other end] under heaven, thus shall the Son of man be in his day. 25 But first he must suffer many things and be rejected of this generation. 26 And **as it took place in the days of Noah**, thus also shall it be in the days of the Son of man: 27 they ate, they drank, they married, they were given in marriage, until the day that Noah entered into the ark, and the flood came and destroyed all [of them]; 28 and in like manner as took place in the days of Lot: they ate, they drank, they bought, they sold, they planted, they builded; 29 but on the day that Lot went out from Sodom, it rained fire and sulphur from heaven, and destroyed all [of them]: 30 after this [manner] shall it be in the day that the Son of man is revealed.

		Luke 17:31 In that day, he who shall be on the housetop, and his stuff in the house, let him not go down to take it away; and he that is in the field, let him likewise not return back. 32 Remember the wife of Lot. 33 Whosoever shall seek to save his life shall lose it, and whosoever shall lose it shall preserve it. 34 I say to you, In that night there shall be two [men] upon one bed; one shall be seized and the other shall be let go. 35 Two [women] shall be grinding together; the one shall be seized and the other shall be let go. 36 [Two men shall be in the field; the one shall be seized and the other let go.]
	Matt 24:28 [For] wherever the carcase is, there will be gathered the eagles.	Luke 17:37 And answering they say to him, Where, Lord? And he said to them, Where the body [is], there the eagles will be gathered together.

The End will come all at once

The End will come at once, as the flood in Noah's day and the destruction of Sodom:	The transgressors destroyed together:	Evil shall not raise again; perpetual peace after the instant destruction:
■ As an overrunning flood (Nah 1:8); ■ speedy riddance (Zeph 1:18); ■ a moment (Ps 73:18); ■ one day (Isa 10:17); ■ in an instant, suddenly (Isa 29:5); ■ destroy and devour at once (Isa 42:14); ■ avenge them speedily (Lk 18:8; Eccl 9:12); ■ one day (rev 18:8); as a whirlwind (Ps 58:9-10); ■ one hour (Rev 18:10, 19); ■ as a flood (Dan 9:26); ■ one day (Isa 47:9); ■ suddenly (1 Thes 5:3); ■ swiftly, speedily (Joel 3:4; Mal 3:5)	■ But transgressors shall be altogether destroyed; the posterity of the wicked shall be cut off. [Psalm 37:38] ■ But rebels and sinners shall be destroyed together, and those who forsake the LORD shall be consumed. [Isaiah 1:28] ■ Then the heavens and the earth, and all that is in them, shall shout for joy over Babylon; for the destroyers shall come against them out of the north, says the LORD. 49 Babylon must fall for the slain of Israel, as the slain of all the earth have fallen because of Babylon. [Jeremiah 51:48]	■ they shall not learn war anymore (Isa 2:4; Mic 4:3); ■ violence no more (Isa 60:18); ■ affliction not to rise a second time (Nah 1:9); ■ shall not see evil anymore (Zeph 3:15); ■ hail will sweep away the lies (Isa 28:17); ■ they shall not hurt nor destroy in all God's holy mountain or kingdom (Isa 11:9); ■ in all God's holy mountain or kingdom, no oppressor shall pass through them anymore (Zech 9:8); ■ God's kingdom and peace will not depart or be removed (Isa 54:10); ■ At Masiah's coming all the kingdoms will be his (Rev 11:15), and there will be no more war as the above scriptures prove.

As in the days of Noah

Matt 24:36 But of that day and hour no one has known,[23] not even the angels of the heavens, but [my] Father alone.

37 But as the days of Noah, so also shall be the coming of the Son of man.

38 For as they were in the days which were before the flood, eating and drinking, marrying and giving in marriage, until the day on which Noah entered into the ark,

39 and they knew not till the flood came and took all away; thus also shall be the coming of the Son of man.

40 Then two shall be in the field, one is taken and one is left;

41 two [women] grinding at the mill, one is taken and one is left.

42 Keep awake therefore, that you do not know in what hour your Lord comes.

43 But know this, that if the master of the house had known in what watch the thief was coming, he would have watched and not have permitted his house to be dug through [into]

44 Wherefore you also, be you ready, that in that hour that you think not the Son of man comes.

Luke 21:34 But take heed to yourselves lest possibly your hearts be laden with surfeiting and drinking and cares of life, and that day come upon you suddenly unawares;

35 for as a snare shall it come upon all them that dwell upon the face of the whole earth.

36 Watch therefore, praying at every season, that you may be accounted worthy to escape all these things which are about to come to pass, and to stand before the Son of man.

Watch

Mark 13:34 [it is] as a man gone out of the country, having left his house and given to his servants the authority, and to each one his work, and commanded the doorkeeper that he should watch.

35 Keep awake therefore, for you have not known[24] when the master of the house comes: evening, or midnight, or cock-crow, or morning;

36 lest coming suddenly he find you sleeping.

37 But what I say to you, I say to all, Keep awake.

Matt 24:45 Who then is the faithful and prudent servant whom his lord has set over his household, to give them food in season?

46 Blessed is that servant whom his lord on coming shall find doing thus.

47 Truly I say unto you, that he will set him over all his substance.

48 But if that evil servant should say in his heart, My lord delays to come,

49 and begin to beat his fellow-servants, and eat and drink with the drunken;

50 the lord of that servant shall come in a day when he does not expect it, and in an hour he knows not of,

51 and shall cut him in two and appoint his portion with the hypocrites: there shall be the weeping and the gnashing of teeth.

Mark 13:35 Keep awake therefore, for you have not known[25] when the master

---

[23] Perfect tense; also perfect tense in Mark 13:32; "The *perfect* conveys the double notion of an action terminated in the past time, and of its effect existing in the present" – Section 39 of the *New Analytical Greek Lexicon*

[24] Perfect tense

[25] Perfect tense; "The *perfect* conveys the double notion of an action terminated in the past time, and of its effect existing in the present" – Section 39 of the *New Analytical Greek Lexicon*

of the house comes: evening, or midnight, or cock-crow, or morning;

36 lest coming suddenly he find you sleeping.

37 But what I say to you, I say to all, Keep awake.

Ten Virgins: Wise and Foolish

Matt 25:1 Then shall the kingdom of the heavens be made like to ten virgins that having taken their torches, went forth to meet the bridegroom.

2 And five of them were prudent and five foolish.

3 They that were foolish took their torches and did not take oil with them;

4 but the prudent took oil in their vessels with their torches.

5 Now the bridegroom tarrying, they all grew heavy and slept.

6 But in the middle of the night there was a cry, Behold, the bridegroom; go forth to meet him.

7 Then all those virgins arose and trimmed their torches.

8 And the foolish said to the prudent, Give us of your oil, for our torches are going out.

9 But the prudent answered saying, [We cannot,] lest it might not suffice for us and for you. Go rather to those that sell, and buy for yourselves.

10 But as they went away to buy, the bridegroom came, and the [ones that were] ready went in with him to the wedding feast, and the door was shut.

11 Afterwards come also the rest of the virgins, saying, Lord, Lord, open to us;

12 but he answering said, Truly I say unto you, I do not know you.

13 Keep awake therefore, that you not know the day nor the hour.

Parable of Talents

14 For [it is] as [if] a man going away out of a country called his own servants and delivered to them his substance.

15 And to one he gave five talents, to another two, and to another one; to each according to his particular ability, and immediately went away out of the country.

16 And he that had received the five talents went and trafficked with them, and made five other talents.

17 In like manner also he that [had received] the two, [he also] gained two others.

18 But he that had received the one went and dug in the earth, and hid the money of his lord.

19 And after a long time the lord of those servants comes and reckons with them.

20 And he that had received the five talents came to him, and brought five other talents, saying, [My] lord, you delivered me five talents; behold, I have gained five other talents besides them.

21 His lord said to him, Well, good and faithful servant, you have been faithful over a few things, I will set you over many things: enter into the joy of thy lord.

22 And he also that had received the two talents came to him, and said, [My] lord, you delivered me two talents; behold, I have gained two other talents besides them.

23 His lord said to him, Well, good and faithful servant, you were faithful over a few things, I will set you over many things: enter you into the joy of thy lord.

24 And he also that had received the one talent coming to him, said, [My] lord, I knew that you are a hard man, reaping where you had not sowed, and

gathering from where you had not scattered;

25 and being afraid I went away and hid thy talent in the earth; behold, you hast that which is thine.

26 And his lord answering said to him, Wicked and slothful servant, you knew that I reap where I had not sowed, and gather from where I had not scattered;

27 you ought then to have put my money to the money-changers, and when I came I should have got what is mine with interest.

28 Take therefore the talent from him, and give it to him that has the ten talents:

29 for to every one that has shall be given, and he shall be in abundance; but from him that has not, that even which he has shall be taken from him.

30 And cast out the useless servant into the outer darkness; there shall be the weeping and the gnashing of teeth.

Last Judgment: Sheep and Goats

31 But when the Son of man comes in his glory, and all the angels with him, then shall he sit down upon his throne of glory

32 and all the nations shall be gathered before him; and he shall separate them from one another, as the shepherd separates the sheep from the goats

33 and he will set the sheep on his right hand, and the goats on [his] left

34 Then shall the King say to those on his right hand, Come, blessed of my Father, inherit the kingdom prepared for you from the world's foundation

35 for I hungered, and you gave me to eat; I thirsted, and you gave me to drink; I was a stranger, and you took me in;

36 naked, and you clothed me; I was ill, and you visited me; I was in prison, and you came to me.

37 Then shall the righteous answer him saying, Lord, when did we see you hungering, and nourished you; or thirsting, and gave you to drink?

38 and when did we see you a stranger, and took you in; or naked, and clothed you?

39 and when did we see you ill, or in prison, and came to you?

40 And the King answering shall say to them, Truly, I say to you, Inasmuch as you have done it to one of the least of these my brethren, you have done it to me.

41 Then shall he say also to those on the left, Go from me, cursed, into aeonian fire, prepared for the devil and his angels:

42 for I hungered, and you gave me not to eat; I thirsted, and you gave me not to drink;

43 I was a stranger, and you took me not in; naked, and you did not clothe me; ill, and in prison, and you did not visit me.

44 Then shall they also answer saying, Lord, when saw we you hungering, or thirsting, or a stranger, or naked, or ill, or in prison, and have not ministered to you?

45 Then shall he answer them saying, Truly I say to you, Inasmuch as you have not done it to one of these least, neither have you done it to me.

46 And these shall go away into aeonian punishment, and the righteous into life aeonian.

Yehoshua Foretells Crucifixion

Matt 26:1 And it came to pass when Yehoshua had finished all these sayings, he said to his disciples,

2 Ye know that after two days the Passover takes place, and the Son of man is delivered up to be crucified.

Conspiracy against Yehoshua

3 Then the chief priests and the elders of the people were gathered together to the palace of the high priest who was called Caiaphas,

4 and took counsel together in order that they might seize Yehoshua by subtlety and kill him;

5 but they said, Not in the feast, that there be not a tumult among the people.

Judas Bargains to Betray Yehoshua

Matt 26:14 Then one of the twelve, he who was called Judas Iscariote, [had went on the 10th] to the chief priest,

15 and said,*, What are you willing to give me, and I will deliver him up to you? And they appointed to him thirty pieces of silver.

16 And from that time [the 10ᵗʰ] he sought a good opportunity that he might deliver him up.

Disbelief and Prophecy

John 12:37 But though he had done so many signs before them, they believed not on him,

38 that the word of the prophet Isaiah which he said might be fulfilled, Lord, who has believed our report? and to whom has the arm of the Lord been revealed?

39 On this account they could not believe, because Isaiah said again,

40 He has blinded their eyes and hardened their heart, that they may not see with their eyes, and understand with their heart and be converted, and I should heal them.

41 These things said Isaiah because he saw his glory and spoke of him.

Some Believed But are Afraid

42 Although indeed from among the rulers also many believed on him, but on account of the Pharisees did not acknowledge him that they might not be put out of the synagogue:

43 for they loved glory from men rather than glory from the God.

Yehoshua Speaks Only What the Father Tells Him

44 But Yehoshua cried and said, He that believes on me, believes not on me, but on him that sent me;

45 and he that beholds me, beholds him that sent me.

46 I am come into the world [as] light, that every one that believes on me may not abide in darkness;

47 and if any one hear my words and do not keep [them] I judge him not, for I am not come that I might judge the world, but that I might save the world.

48 He that rejects me and does not receive my words, has him who judges him: the word which I have spoken, that shall judge him in the last day.

49 For I have not spoken from myself, but the Father who sent me has himself given me commandment what I should say and what I should speak;

50 and I know that his commandment is aeonian life. What therefore I speak, as the Father has said to me, so I speak.

13ᵗʰ of Nisan, a Tuesday

Disciples Prepare for the Passover

Luke 22:7 And towards the day of unleavened bread came, in which the Passover was to be killed.

8 And he sent Peter and John, saying, Go and prepare the Passover for us, that we may eat it

9 But they said to him, Where will you that we prepare it

10 And he said to them, Behold, as you enter into the city a man will meet you,

carrying an earthen pitcher of water; follow him into the house where he goes in;

11 and you shall say to the master of the house, The Teacher says to you, Where is the guest-chamber where I may eat the Passover with my disciples?

12 And he will show you a large upper room furnished: there make ready.

13 And having gone they found it as he had said to them; and they prepared* the Passover.

Evening of the 13th of Nisan

Last Supper

14 And when the hour was come, he placed himself at table, and the [twelve] apostles with him.

15 And he said to them, With desire I have desired this Passover to eat with you before I suffer.

16 Since I say unto you, that I will not eat it [Passover] until it be fulfilled in the kingdom of the God.

17 And having received a cup, when he had given thanks he said, Take this and divide it among yourselves.

18 For I say unto you, that I will not drink at all of the fruit of the vine until the kingdom of the God come.

19 And having taken a loaf, when he had given thanks, he broke it and gave it to them, saying, This is my body which is given for you: this do in remembrance of me.

20 In like manner also the cup, after having supper, saying, This cup [is] the new covenant in my blood, which is poured out for you.

21 Moreover, behold, the hand of him that delivers me up [is] with me on the table;

22 and the Son of man indeed goes as it is determined, but woe unto that man by whom he is delivered up.

23 And they began to question together among themselves who then it could be of them who was about to do this.

24 And there was also a strife among them which of them should be held to be the greatest.

25 And he said to them, The kings of the nations rule over them, and they that exercise authority over them are called benefactors.

26 But you [shall] not [be] thus; but let the greater among you be as the younger, and the leader as he that serves.

27 For which [is] greater, he that is at table or he that serves? [is] not he that is at table? But I am in the midst of you as the one that serves.

28 But you are they who have persevered with me in my testing.

29 And I appoint unto you, as my Father has appointed unto me, a kingdom,

30 that you may eat and drink at my table in my kingdom, and sit on thrones judging the twelve tribes of Israel.

Yehoshua Washes Apostles' Feet

John 13:1 Now before the feast of the Passover, Yehoshua, knowing that his hour had come that he should depart out of this world to the Father, having loved his own who were in the world, loved them to the end.

2 And during supper, the evil mind [daemon] having already put it into the heart of Judas [son] of Simon, Iscariote, that he should deliver him up,

3 [Yehoshua,] knowing that the Father had given him all things into his hands,

and that he came out from God and was going toward the God,

4 rises from supper and lays aside his garments, and having taken a linen towel he girded himself:

5 then he pours water into the wash-hand basin, and began to wash the feet of the disciples, and to wipe them with the linen towel with which he was girded.

6 He comes therefore to Simon Peter; and he says to him, Lord, do you wash my feet?

7 Yehoshua answered and said to him, What I do you do not know now, but you shall know hereafter.

8 Peter says to him, You shall never wash my feet. Yehoshua answered him, Unless I wash you, you have no part with me.

9 Simon Peter says to him, Lord, not my feet only, but also my hands and my head.

10 Yehoshua says to him, He that is washed all over needs not to wash except his feet, but is wholly clean; and you are clean, but not all.

11 For he knew him that delivered him up: on account of this he said, You are not all clean.

12 When therefore he had washed their feet, and taken his garments, having sat down again, he said to them, Do you know what I have done to you?

13 You call me the Teacher and the Lord, and you say well, for I am [so].

14 If I therefore, the Lord and the Teacher, have washed your feet, you also ought to wash one another's feet;

15 for I have given you an example that, as I have done to you, you should do also.

16 Truly, truly, I say to you, The servant is not greater than his lord, nor the sent greater than he who has sent him.

17 If you know these things, blessed are you if you do them.

Yehoshua Foretells Betrayal

18 I speak not of you all. I know those whom I have chosen; but that the scripture might be fulfilled, He that eats bread with me has lifted up his heel against me.

19 I tell you it now before it happens, that when it happens, you may believe that I am he.

20 Truly, truly, I say to you, He who receives whomsoever I shall send receives me; and he that receives me receives him who has sent me.

21 Having said these things, Yehoshua was troubled in spirit, and testified and said, Truly, truly, I say to you, that one of you shall deliver me up.

22 The disciples therefore looked one on another, uncertain of whom he spoke.

23 Now there was at table one of his disciples in the bosom of Yehoshua, whom Yehoshua loved.

24 Simon Peter makes a sign therefore to him to ask who it might be of whom he spoke.

25 But he, leaning on the breast of Yehoshua, says to him, Lord, who is it?

26 Yehoshua answers, He it is to whom I, after I have dipped the morsel, give it. And having dipped the morsel, he gives it to Judas [son] of Simon, Iscariote.

27 And, after the morsel, then entered Satan into him. Yehoshua therefore says to him, What you do, do quickly.

28 But none of those at table knew why he said this to him;

29 for some supposed, because Judas had the bag, that Yehoshua was saying to him, Buy the things of which we have

need for the feast; or that he should give something to the poor.

Night of the 14th, a Wednesday

30 Having therefore received the morsel, he went out immediately; and it was night.

31 When therefore he had gone out Yehoshua says, Now is the Son of man glorified,* and the God is glorified* in him [Son of man].

32 If the God be glorified* in him, now the God also will glorify [fut] Himself in him [Son of man], and will glorify [fut] Himself immediately.

33 Children, yet a little while I am with you. You shall seek me; and, as I said to the Jews, Where I go you cannot come, I say to you also now.

New Commandment

34 A new commandment I give to you, that you love one another; as I have loved you, that you also love one another.

35 By this shall all know that you are disciples of mine, if you have love among yourselves.

36 Simon Peter says to him, Lord, where are you going? Yehoshua answered him, Where I go you can not follow me now, but you shall follow me after.

37 Peter says to him, Lord, why cannot I follow you now? I will lay down my soul for you.

38 Yehoshua answers, You will lay down your soul for me! Truly, truly, I say to you, The cock shall not crow till you have denied me three times.

Lord, Where are You Going

John 14:1 Let not your heart be troubled; you believe on the God, believe also on me.

2 In my Father's house there are many abodes; were it not so, I had told you: for I go to prepare you a place;

3 and if I go and shall prepare you a place, I am coming again and shall receive you to myself, that where I am you also may be.

4 And you know where I go, and you know the way.

5 Thomas says to him, Lord, we know not where you are going, and how can we know the way?

6 Yehoshua says to him, I am the way, and the truth, and the life. No one comes to the Father unless by me.

7 If you had known me, you would have known also my Father, and henceforth you know him and have seen him.

Philip: Show us the Father

8 Philip says to him, Lord, show us the Father and it suffices us.

9 Yehoshua says to him, Am I so long a time with you, and you have not known me, Philip? He that has seen me has seen the Father; and how can you say, Show us the Father?

10 Don't you believe that I am in the Father, and that the Father is in me? The words which I speak to you I do not speak from myself; but the Father who abides in me, he does the works.

11 Believe me that I am in the Father and the Father in me; but if not, believe me for the works' sake themselves.

12 Truly, truly, I say to you, He that believes on me, the works which I do shall he shall do also, and he shall do greater than these, because I go to the Father.

13 And whatsoever you shall ask in my name, this will I do, that the Father may be glorified in the Son.

14 If you shall ask anything in my name, I will do it.

15 If you love me, keep my commandments.

Promise of the Holy Spirit

16 And I will ask the Father, and he will give you another Comforter, that he may be with you into the aeon,

17 the Spirit of truth, whom the world cannot receive, because it does not see him nor know him; but you know him, for he abides with you, and shall be in you.

18 I will not leave you orphans, I am coming to you.

19 Yet a little and the world sees me no longer; but you see me; because I live you also shall live.

20 In that day you shall know that I am in my Father, and you in me, and I in you.

21 He that has my commandments and keeps them, he it is that loves me; but he that loves me shall be loved by my Father, and I will love him and will manifest myself to him.

Why isn't Yehoshua Manifested to the World

22 Judas, not the Iscariot, says to him, Lord, how is it that you will manifest yourself to us and not to the world?

23 Yehoshua answered and said to him, If any one love me, he will keep my word, and my Father will love him, and we will come to him and make our abode with him.

24 He that loves me not does not keep my words; and the word which you hear is not mine, but that of the Father who has sent me.

Yehoshua Promises to send the Holy Spirit

25 These things I have said to you, abiding with you;

26 but the Comforter, the Holy Spirit, whom the Father will send in my name, he shall teach you all things, and will bring to your remembrance all the things which I have said to you.

27 I leave peace with you; I give my peace to you: not as the world gives do I give to you. Let not your heart be troubled, neither let it fear.

28 You have heard that I have said unto you, I go away and I am coming to you. If you loved me you would rejoice that I go to the Father, for [my] Father is greater than I.

29 And now I have told you before it comes to pass, that when it shall have come to pass you may believe.

30 I will no longer speak much with you, for the ruler of the world comes, and in me he has nothing;

31 but that the world may know that I love the Father, and as the Father has commanded me, thus I do. Rise up, let us go from here.

Yehoshua to Fulfill More Prophecy

Luke 22:35 And he said to them, When I sent you without purse and scrip and sandals, did you lack anything? And they said, Nothing.

36 He said therefore to them, But now he that has a purse let him take it in like manner also a scrip, and he that has none let him sell his garment and buy a sword;

37 for I say unto you, that this that is written must yet be accomplished in me, And he was reckoned with the lawless: for also the things concerning me have a fulfillment.

38 And they said, Lord, behold here are two swords. And he said to them, It is enough.

Back to the Mount of Olives

Matt 26:30 And having sung a hymn, they went out to the mount of Olives.

Yehoshua Foretells that the Apostles will Forsake Him

Matt 26:31 Then says Yehoshua to them, All of you shall be offended in me during this night. For it is written, I will smite the shepherd, and the sheep of the flock shall be scattered abroad

32 But after that I shall be risen, I will go before you to Galilee.

33 And Peter answering said to him, If all shall be offended in you, I will never be offended.

34 Yehoshua said to him, Truly I say to you, that during this night, before the cock shall crow, you shall deny me three times.

35 Peter says to him, If I should needs die with you, I will in no wise deny you. Likewise said all the disciples also.

Vine and the Branches

John 15:1 I am the true vine, and my Father is the husbandman.

2 [As to] every branch in me not bearing fruit, he takes it away; and [as to] every one bearing fruit, he prunes it that it may bring forth more fruit.

3 You are already clean by reason of the word which I have spoken to you.

4 Abide in me and I in you. As the branch cannot bear fruit of itself unless it abide in the vine, thus neither [can] you unless you abide in me.

5 I am the vine, you [are] the branches. He that abides in me and I in him, he bears much fruit; for without me you can do nothing.

6 Unless any one abide in me he is cast out as the branch, and is dried up; and they gather them and cast them into the fire, and they are burned.

7 If you abide in me, and my words abide in you, you shall ask what you will and it shall come to pass to you.

8 In this is my Father glorified, that you bear much fruit, and you shall become disciples of mine.

Love One Another

9 As the Father has loved me, I also have loved you: abide in my love.

10 If you shall keep my commandments, you shall abide in my love, as I have kept my Father's commandments and abide in his love.

11 I have spoken these things to you that my joy may be in you, and your joy be full.

12 This is my commandment, that you love one another, as I have loved you.

13 No one has greater love than this, that one should lay down his soul for his friends.

14 You are my friends if you practice whatever I command you.

15 I call you no longer servants, for the servant does not know what his master is doing; but I have called you friends, for all things which I have heard of my Father I have made known to you.

16 You have not chosen me, but I have chosen you, and have set you that you should go and that you should bear fruit, and that your fruit should abide, that whatsoever you shall ask the Father in my name he may give you.

17 These things I command you, that you love one another.

If They Hate Yehoshua They Will Hate You

18 If the world hates you, know that it has hated me before you.

19 If you were of the world, the world would love its own; but because you

are not of the world, but I have chosen you out of the world, on account of this the world hates you.

20 Remember the word which I said unto you, The servant is not greater than his master. If they have persecuted me, they will also persecute you; if they have kept my word, they will keep also yours.

21 But they will do all these things to you on account of my name, because they have not known him that sent me.

22 If I had not come and spoken to them, they would have no sin; but now they have no excuse for their sin.

23 He that hates me hates also my Father.

24 If I had not done among them the works which no other one has done, they had not had sin; but now they have both seen and hated both me and my Father.

25 But that the word written in their law might be fulfilled, They hated me without a cause.

26 But when the Comforter is come, whom I will send to you from the Father, the Spirit of truth who goes forth from the Father, he shall bear witness concerning me;

27 and you too bear witness, because you are with me from the beginning.

John 16:1 These things I have spoken unto you that you may not be offended.

2 They shall put you out of the synagogues; but the hour is coming that every one who kills you will think to render service to the God;

3 and these things they will do because they have not known the Father nor me.

4 But I have spoken these things to you, that when their hour shall have come, you may remember them, that I have said [them] unto you. But I did not say these things unto you from the beginning, because I was with you.

Yehoshua Had to go Away

5 But now I go to him that has sent me, and none of you asks of me, Where do you go?

6 But because I have spoken these things to you, sorrow has filled your heart.

7 But I say the truth to you, It is profitable for you that I go away; for if I do not go away, the Comforter will not come to you; but if I go I will send him to you.

8 And having come, he will reprove the world concerning sin, and concerning righteousness, and concerning judgment:

9 of sin, because they do not believe on me;

10 of righteousness, because I go away to my Father, and you behold me no longer;

11 of judgment, because the ruler of this world is judged.

Spirit of Truth To Teach You

12 I have yet many things to say to you, but you cannot bear them now.

13 But when he is come, the Spirit of truth, he shall guide you into all the truth: for he shall not speak from himself; but whatsoever he shall hear he shall speak; and he will announce to you what is coming.

14 He shall glorify me, for he shall receive of mine and shall announce it to you.

15 All things that the Father has are mine; on account of this I have said that he receives of mine and shall announce it to you.

Disciples Don't Understand Where Yehoshua Was Going

16 A little while and you do not behold me; and again a little while and you shall see me, [because I go away to the father]

17 [Some] of his disciples therefore said to one another, What is this he says to us, A little while and you do not behold me; and again a little while and you shall see me, and, Because I go away toward the Father?

18 They said therefore, What is this which he says of the little while? We do not know of what he speaks.

19 Yehoshua knew therefore that they desired to ask of him, and said to them, Do you inquire of this among yourselves that I said, A little while and you do not behold me; and again a little while and you shall see me?

20 Truly, truly, I say to you, that you shall weep and lament, you, but the world shall rejoice; and you will be grieved, but your grief shall be turned to joy.

21 A woman, when she gives birth to a child, has grief because her hour has come; but when the child is born, she no longer remembers the trouble, on account of the joy that a man has been born into the world.

22 And you now therefore have grief; but I will see you again, and your heart shall rejoice, and your joy no one takes from you.

23 And in that day you shall ask nothing of me: truly, truly, I say to you, Whatsoever you shall ask the Father in my name, he will give you.

24 Until now you have asked nothing in my name: ask, and you shall receive, that your joy may be full.

In the Future Yehoshua Will Teach Without Parables

25 These things I have spoken to you in parables; the hour is coming that I will no longer speak to you in parables, but will declare to you openly concerning the Father.

26 In that day you shall ask in my name; and I say not to you that I will ask of the Father for you,

27 for the Father himself has affection for you, because you have had affection for me, and have believed that I came out from the God.

28 I came out from the Father and have come into the world; again, I leave the world and go toward the Father.

29 His disciples say to him, Lo, now you speak openly and utter no parable.

30 Now we know that you know all things, and have not need that any one should ask of you. By this we believe that you are come from God.

31 Yehoshua answered them, Do you now believe?

32 Behold, the hour is coming, and has come, that you shall be scattered, each to his own, and shall leave me alone; and [yet] I am not alone, for the Father is with me.

33 These things have I spoken to you that in me you might have peace. In the world you have tribulation; but be of good courage: I have overcome the world.

Yehoshua Prays for All

John 17:1 These things Yehoshua spoke, and lifted up his eyes to heaven and said, Father, the hour is come; glorify your Son, that your Son may glorify you;

2 as you have given him authority over all flesh, that [as to] all that you have given to him, he should give them aeonian life.

3 And this is the aeonian life, that they should know you, the only true God, and Yehoshua Masiah whom you have sent.

4 I have glorified you on the earth, I have completed the work which you gave me that I should do it;

5 and now glorify me, you Father, beside yourself,[26] with the glory which I possessed[27] before the world, to be beside you[28].

6 I have manifested your name to the men whom you gave me out of the world. They were yours, and you gave them to me, and they have kept your word.

7 Now they have known that all things that you have given me are from you;

8 for the words which you have given me I have given them, and they have received [them] and have known truly that I came out from you, and have believed that you sent me.

9 I ask concerning them; I do not ask concerning the world, but concerning those whom you have given me, for they are yours,

10 and all that is mine is yours, and [all] that is yours is mine, and I am glorified in them.

11 And I am no longer in the world, and these are in the world, and I come to you. Holy Father, keep them in your name which you have given me, that they may be one as we.

12 When I was with them I kept them in your name; those you have given me I have guarded, and not one of them has perished, but the son of perdition, that the scripture might be fulfilled.

13 And now I come to you. And these things I speak in the world, that they may have my joy fulfilled in them.

14 I have given them your word, and the world has hated them, because they are not of the world, as I am not of the world.

15 I do not ask that you should take them out of the world, but that you should keep them out of evil.

16 They are not of the world, as I am not of the world.

17 Sanctify them by the truth: your word is truth.

18 As you have sent me into the world, I also have sent them into the world;

19 and I sanctify myself for them, that they also may be sanctified by truth.

20 And I do not ask for these only, but also for those who believe on me through their word;

21 that they may be all one, as you, Father, are in me, and I in you, that they also may be one in us, that the world may believe that you have sent me.

22 And the glory which you have given me I have given them, that they may be one, as we are one;

23 I in them and you in me, that they may be perfected into one [and] that the world may know that you have sent me, and that you have loved them as you have loved me.

24 Father, [as to] those whom you have given me, I desire that where I am they also may be with me, that they may behold my glory which you have given me, for you loved me before the foundation of the world.

25 Righteous Father, – and the world has not known you, but I have known you, and these have known that you have sent me.

---

[26] On the Right Side of God (Psalm 110:1)

[27] Incomplete verb, thus he possessed something before the world was, but at the time of him speaking, it was not yet fully possessed.

[28] As the Right Side of God

26 And I have made known to them your name, and will make it known; that the love with which you have loved me may be in them and I in them.

Yehoshua prays in the Garden

John 18:1 Yehoshua, having said these things, went out with his disciples beyond the brook Kidron, where was a garden, into which he entered, he and his disciples.

Mark 14:32 And they come to a place of which the name [is] Gethsemane, and he says to his disciples, Sit here while I shall pray.

33 And he takes with him Peter and James and John, and he began to be amazed and oppressed in spirit.

34 And he says to them, My soul is full of grief even unto death; abide here and keep awake.

Yehoshua Prays Again

Luke 22:41 And he was withdrawn from them about a stone's throw, and having knelt down he prayed,

42 saying, Father, if you will remove this cup from me: – but then, not my will, but yours be done.

43 And an angel appeared to him from heaven strengthening him.

44 And being in conflict he prayed more intently. And his sweat became as great drops of blood, falling down upon the earth.

45 And rising up from his prayer, coming to the disciples, he found them sleeping from grief.

Matt 26:40 And he comes to the disciples and finds them sleeping, and says to Peter, Thus you have not been able to watch one hour with me?

41 Keep awake and pray, that you enter not into temptation: the spirit indeed [is] ready, but the flesh weak.

42 Again going away a second time he prayed saying, My Father, if this cannot pass [from me] unless I drink it, thy will be done.

43 And coming he found them again sleeping, for their eyes were heavy.

44 And leaving them, he went away again and prayed the third time, saying the same thing.

45 Then he comes to the disciples and says to them, Sleep on now and take your rest; behold, the hour has drawn nigh, and the Son of man is delivered up into the hands of sinners.

46 Arise, let us go; behold, he that delivers me up has drawn near.

Judas Betrays Yehoshua With a Kiss

John 18:2 And Judas also, who delivered him up, knew the place, because Yehoshua was often there, in company with his disciples.

3 Judas therefore, having got the band, and officers of the chief priests and Pharisees, comes there with lanterns and torches and weapons.

Mark 14:43 And immediately, while he [Yehoshua] was yet speaking, Judas comes up, [being] one of the twelve, and with him a great crowd, with swords and sticks, from the chief priests and the scribes and the elders.

44 Now he [Judas] that delivered him [Yehoshua] up had given them a sign between them, saying, Whomsoever I shall kiss, that is he; seize him, and lead him away safely.

45 And being come, straightway coming up to him, he says, Rabbi, Rabbi; and he covered him with kisses.

Luke 22:48 And Yehoshua said to him, Judas, do you deliver up the Son of man with a kiss?

John 18:4 Yehoshua therefore, knowing all things that were coming upon him, went forth and said to them, Whom do you seek?

5 They answered him, Yehoshua the Nazarene. Yehoshua says to them, I am he. And Judas also, who delivered him up, stood with them.

6 When therefore he said to them, I am he, they went away backward and fell to the ground.

7 He asked of them therefore again, Whom do you seek? And they said, Yehoshua the Nazarene.

8 Yehoshua answered, I told you that I am he, if therefore you seek me, let these go away;

9 that the word might be fulfilled which he spoke, [as to] those whom you have given me, I have not lost one of them.

Peter Cuts Off Ear of the Servant of the High Priest

10 Simon Peter therefore, having a sword, drew it, and smote the servant of the high priest and cut off his right ear; and the servant's name was Malchus.

Luke 22::51 And Yehoshua answering said, Stop, no more of this -- and having touched his ear, he healed him.

John 18:11 Yehoshua therefore said to Peter, Put the sword into the sheath; the cup which the Father has given me, shall I not drink it?

Matt 26:53 Or think you that I cannot now call upon my Father, and he will furnish me more than twelve legions of angels?

54 How then should the scriptures be fulfilled that thus it must be?

Yehoshua Arrested

Luke 22:52 And Yehoshua said to the chief priests and captains of the temple and elders, who were come against him, Have you come out as against a robber with swords and sticks?

53 When I was day by day with you in the temple you did not stretch out your hands against me; but this is your hour and the power of darkness.

Matt 26:56 But all this is come to pass that the scriptures of the prophets may be fulfilled. Then all the disciples left him and fled.

Mark 14:50 And all left him and fled.

51 And a certain young man followed him with a linen cloth cast about his naked [body] and [the young men] seize him;

52 but he, leaving the linen cloth behind him, fled from them naked.

John 18:12 The band therefore, and the centurions, and the officers of the Jews, took Yehoshua and bound him:

Yehoshua Taken to Annas (Former High Priest)

13 and they led him away to Annas first; for he was father-in- law to Caiaphas, who was high priest that year.

14 But it was Caiaphas who counseled the Jews that it was better that one man should perish for the people.

Peter Denies Yehoshua

15 Now Simon Peter followed Yehoshua, and the other disciple. But that disciple was known to the high priest, and went in with Yehoshua into the palace of the high priest;

16 but Peter stood at the door outside. The other disciple therefore, who was known to the high priest, went out and spoke to the female-doorkeeper and brought in Peter.

17 The maid therefore, who was the female-doorkeeper, says to Peter, Are you also of the disciples of this man? He says, I am not.

18 But the servants and officers, having made a fire of coals for it was cold, stood and warmed themselves; and Peter was standing with them and warming himself.

Yehoshua Before the High Priest

19 The high priest therefore asked of Yehoshua concerning his disciples and concerning his doctrine.

20 Yehoshua answered him, I spoke openly to the world; I taught always in the synagogue and in the temple, where all the Jews come together, and in secret I have spoken nothing.

21 Why do you ask me? Ask those who have heard, what I have spoken to them; look, they know what I have said.

22 But as he said these things, one of the officers who stood by gave a blow on the face to Yehoshua, saying, Answer you the high priest thus?

23 Yehoshua answered him, If I have spoken evil, bear witness of the evil; but if well, why do you hit me?

Yehoshua Sent to Caiaphas, the High Priest

John 18:24 Annas [then] had sent him bound to Caiaphas the high priest.

Luke 22:54 And having laid hold on him, they led him [away] and they led him into the house of the high priest. And Peter followed afar off.

Peter Denies Yehoshua Again

55 And they having lit a fire in the midst of the court and sat down together, Peter sat among them.

56 And a certain maid, having seen him sitting by the light, and having fixed her eyes upon him, said, And this [man] was with him.

57 But he denied him, saying, Woman, I do not know him.

58 And after a short time another seeing him said, And you are of them. But Peter said, Man, I am not.

Yehoshua Before Caiaphas and the Sanhedrin

Mark 14:55 And the chief priests and the whole Sanhedrim sought testimony against Yehoshua to cause him to be put to death, and did not find [any]

56 For many bore false witness against him, and their testimony did not agree.

57 And certain persons rose up and bore false witness against him, saying,

58 We heard him saying, I will destroy this temple which is made with hands, and in the course of three days I will build another not made with hands.

59 And neither thus did their testimony agree.

60 And the high priest, rising up before them all, asked Yehoshua, saying, Answer you nothing? What do these testify against you?

61 But he was silent, and answered nothing. Again the high priest asked him, and says to him, Are you the Masiah, the Son of the Blessed?

62 And Yehoshua said, I am, and you shall see the Son of man sitting at the right hand of power, and coming with the clouds of heaven.

63 And the high priest, having rent his clothes, says, What need have we any more of witnesses?

64 You have heard the blasphemy; what do you think? And they all condemned him to be guilty of death.

65 And some began to spit upon him, and cover up his face, and hit him, and say to him, Prophesy; and the officers struck him with the palms of their hands.

Peter Denies Yehoshua Third Time

Matt 26:73 And after a little, those who stood [there], coming to him, said to Peter, Truly you too are of them, for also thy speech makes you manifest.

Luke 22:59 And after the lapse of about one hour another stoutly maintained it, saying, In truth this [man] also was with him, for also he is a Galilaean.

Matt 26:74 Then he began to curse and to swear, I know not the man. And immediately the cock crew.

Luke 22:61 And the Lord, turning round, looked at Peter; and Peter remembered the word of the Lord, how he said to him, Before the cock crow you shall deny me three times.

62 And Peter, going forth outside, wept bitterly.

Council Condemns Yehoshua

Luke 22:66 And when it was day, the elderhood of the people, both the chief priests and scribes, were gathered together, and led him into their council, saying,

67 If you are the Masiah, tell us. And he said to them, If I tell you, you will not at all believe;

68 and if I should ask [you] you would not answer me at all, nor let me go;

69 but henceforth shall the Son of man be sitting on the right hand of the power of the God.

70 And they all said, You then are the Son of the God? And he said to them, You say that I am.

71 And they said, What need have we any more of witness, for we have heard ourselves out of his mouth?

Matt 27:1 And when it was morning all the chief priests and the elders of the people took counsel against Yehoshua so that they might put him to death.

Yehoshua Bound and Taken to Pontius Pilate, the Governor

2 And having bound him they led him away, and delivered him up to Pontius Pilate, the governor.

Judas Commits Suicide; 30 Pieces of Silver

3 Then Judas, who delivered him up, seeing that he had been condemned, filled with remorse, returned the thirty pieces of silver to the chief priests and the elders,

4 saying, I have sinned [in] having delivered up guiltless blood. But they said, What is that to us? see you [to that].

5 And having cast down the pieces of silver in the temple, he left the place, and went away and hanged himself.

6 And the chief priests took the pieces of silver and said, It is not lawful to cast them into the Corban, since it is the price of blood.

7 And having taken counsel, they bought with them the field of the potter for a burying-ground for strangers.

8 Wherefore that field has been called Blood-field unto this day.

9 Then was fulfilled that which was spoken through Jeremiah the prophet, saying, And I took the thirty pieces of silver, the price of him that was set a price on, whom [they who were] of the sons of Israel had set a price on,

10 and they gave them for the field of the potter, according as the Lord commanded me.

Yehoshua Before Pilate

John 18:28 [Luke 23:1] They lead therefore Yehoshua from Caiaphas to the praetorium; and it was early morn. And they entered not into the praetorium, that they might not be defiled, but eat the Passover.

29 Pilate therefore went out to them and said, What accusation do you bring against this man?

30 They answered and said to him, If this [man] were not an evildoer, we should not have delivered him up to you.

John 18:31 Pilate therefore said to them, Take him, you, and judge him according to your law. The Jews therefore said to him, It is not permitted to us to put any one to death;

32 (that the word of Yehoshua might be fulfilled which he spoke, signifying what death he should die).

Luke 23:2 And they began to accuse him, saying, We have found this [man] perverting our nation, and forbidding to give tribute to Caesar, saying that he himself is Masiah, a king.

Pilate Questions Yehoshua

John 18:33 Pilate therefore entered again into the praetorium and called Yehoshua, and said to him, Are you the king of the Jews?

34 Yehoshua answered him. Do you say this of yourself, or have others said it to you concerning me?

35 Pilate answered, Am I a Jew? Your nation and the chief priests have delivered you up to me: what have you done?

36 Yehoshua answered, My kingdom is not of this world; if my kingdom were of this world, my servants had fought that I might not be delivered up to the Jews; but now my kingdom is not from hence.

37 Pilate therefore said to him, You are then a king? Yehoshua answered, You say it that I am a king. I have been born for this, and for this I have come into the world, that I might bear witness to the truth. Every one that is of the truth hears my voice.

38 Pilate says to him, What is truth? And having said this he went out again to the Jews, and says to them, I find no fault whatever in him.

Yehoshua Sent to Herod; Sent Back to Pilate

Luke 23:5 But they insisted, saying, He stirs up the people, teaching throughout all Judea, beginning from Galilee even on to here.

6 But Pilate, having heard Galilee [named] asked if the man were a Galilaean;

7 and having learned that he was of Herod's jurisdiction, he sent him to Herod, who himself also was at Jerusalem in those days.

8 And when Herod saw Yehoshua he greatly rejoiced, for he had been a long while desirous of seeing him, because of hearing many things concerning him, and he hoped to see some sign done by him;

9 and he questioned him in many words, but he answered him nothing.

10 And the chief priests and the scribes stood and accused him violently.

11 And Herod with his troops having set him at nought and mocked him, having put a splendid robe upon him, sent him back to Pilate.

12 And Pilate and Herod became friends with one another the same day, for they had been at enmity before between themselves.

Matt 27:19 But, as he was sitting on the judgment-seat, his [Pilate's] wife sent to him, saying, Have you nothing to do with that righteous [man]; for I have suffered to-day many things in a dream because of him.

Yehoshua Before Pilate Again

Luke 23:13 And Pilate, having called together the chief priests and the rulers and the people,

14 said to them, You have brought to me this man as turning away the people [to rebellion] and behold, I, having examined him before you, have found nothing criminal in this man as to the things of which you accuse him;

15 nor Herod either, for he sent him back to us, for nothing worthy of death was done by him.

16 Having chastised him therefore, I will release him.

Yehoshua and Barabbas

Mark 15:6 But at the feast he released to them one prisoner, whomsoever they begged [of him].

7 Now there was the [person] named Barabbas bound with those who had made insurrection with him [and] that had committed murder in the insurrection.

8 And the crowd crying out began to beg [that he would do] to them as he had always done.

9 But Pilate answered them saying, Do you wish that I release to you the King of the Jews?

10 for he knew that the chief priests had delivered him up through envy.

11 But the chief priests stirred up the crowd that he might rather release Barabbas to them.

Matt 27:21 And the governor answering said to them, Which of the two will you that I release unto you? And they said, Barabbas.

Luke 23:18 But they cried out in a mass saying, Away with this [man] and release Barabbas to us;

John 18:40 They cried therefore again all, saying, Not this [Yehoshua] but Barabbas. Now Barabbas was a robber.

Luke 23:19 who was one who, for a certain tumult which had taken place in the city, and [for] murder, had been cast into prison.

20 Pilate therefore, desirous to release Yehoshua, again addressed [them]

21 But they cried out in reply saying, Crucify, crucify him.

22 And he said the third time to them, What evil then has this [man] done? I have found no cause of death in him: I will chastise him therefore and release him.

23 But they were urgent with loud voices, begging that he might be crucified. And their voices [and those of the chief priests] prevailed.

Matt 27:27 Then the soldiers of the governor, having taken Yehoshua with [them] to the praetorium, gathered against him the whole band,

28 and having taken off his garment, put on him a scarlet cloak,

29 and having woven a crown out of thorns, they put it on his head, and a reed in his right hand; and, bowing the knee before him, they mocked him, saying, Hail, King of the Jews.

30 And having spit upon him, they took the reed and beat him on his head.

John 19:4 And Pilate went out again and says to them, Lo, I bring him out to you, that you may know that I find in him no fault whatever.

5 Yehoshua therefore went forth outside, wearing the crown of thorns, and the purple robe. And he says to them, Look at the man!

6 When therefore the chief priests and the officers saw him they cried out saying, Crucify, crucify him. Pilate says to them, You take him and crucify him, but I find no fault in him.

7 The Jews answered him, We have a law, and according to [our] law he ought to die, because he made himself Son of God.

8 When Pilate therefore heard this word, he was afraid,

9 and went into the praetorium again and says to Yehoshua, Who are you? But Yehoshua gave him no answer.

10 Pilate therefore says to him, You speak not to me? Do you not know that I have authority to release you and have authority to crucify you?

11 Yehoshua answered, You have no authority whatever against me if it

were not given to you from above. On this account he that has delivered me up to you has the greater sin.

12 From this time Pilate sought to release him; but the Jews cried out saying, If you release this [man] you are not a friend to Caesar. Every one making himself a king speaks against Caesar.

13 Pilate therefore, having heard these words, led Yehoshua out and sat down upon the judgment-seat, at a place called Pavement, but in Hebrew

Gabbatha;

6 *A.M. on the 14th of Nisan*

14 now it was the preparation of the Passover; it was about the sixth hour [6 a.m., Roman time]; and he says to the Jews, Behold your king!

15 But they cried out, Take him away, take him away, crucify him. Pilate says to them, Shall I crucify your king? The chief priests answered, We have no king but Caesar.

Pilate Washes Hands

Matt 27:24 And Pilate, seeing that it availed nothing, but that rather a tumult was arising, having taken water, washed his hands before the crowd, saying, I am guiltless of the blood of this righteous one: see you [to it].

Jews say, His Blood on Us and Our Children

Matt 27:25 And all the people answering said, His blood [be] on us and on our children.

Barabbas Released; Yehoshua to Crucifixion

Luke 23:24 And Pilate adjudged that what they begged should take place.

25 And he released him who, for tumult and murder, had been cast into prison, whom they begged for, and Yehoshua he delivered up to their will.

Mark 15:20 And when they had mocked him, they took the purple off him, and put his own clothes on him; and they lead him out that they may crucify him.

John 19:17 And he went out, bearing his cross, to the place called [place] of a skull, which is called in Hebrew, Golgotha;

Yehoshua Helped by Simon in Carrying the Cross

Mark 15:21 And they compel to go [with them] a certain passer-by, Simon, a Cyrenian, coming from the field, the father of Alexander and Rufus, that he might carry his cross.

22 And they bring him to the place [called] Golgotha, which, being interpreted, is Place of a skull.

Women Weep

Luke 23:27 And a great multitude of the people, and of women who wailed and lamented him, followed him.

28 And Yehoshua turning round to them said, Daughters of Jerusalem, do not weep over me, but weep over yourselves and over your children;

29 for behold, days are coming in which they will say, Blessed [are] the barren, and wombs that have not borne, and breasts that have not given suck.

30 Then shall they begin to say to the mountains, Fall upon us; and to the hills, Cover us:

31 for if these things are done in the green tree, what shall take place in the dry? 9 A.M. on the 14th of Nisan

Yehoshua Crucified

32 Now two others also, malefactors, were led with him to be put to death.

33 And when they came to the place which is called Skull, there they crucified him, and the malefactors, one on the right hand, the other on the left.

34 And Yehoshua said, Father, forgive them, for they know not what they do.

Mark 15:23 And they offered him wine [to drink] medicated with myrrh; but he did not take it

25 And it was the third hour [Jewish time or 9 a.m.], and they crucified him.

Inscription on Cross

John 19:19 And Pilate wrote a title also and put it on the cross. But there was written: Yehoshua the Nazarene, the King of the Jews.

20 This title therefore many of the Jews read, for the place of the city where Yehoshua was crucified was near; and it was written in Hebrew, Greek, Latin.

21 The chief priests of the Jews therefore said to Pilate, Do not write, The king of the Jews, but that he said, I am king of the Jews.

22 Pilate answered, What I have written, I have written.

Soldiers Cast Lots

23 The soldiers therefore, when they had crucified Yehoshua, took his clothes, and made four parts, to each soldier a part, and the body-coat; but the body-coat was seamless, woven through the whole from the top.

24 They said therefore to one another, Let us not rip it, but let us cast lots for it, whose it shall be; that the scripture might be fulfilled which says,

> They parted my garments among themselves, and on my vesture they cast lots. The soldiers therefore did these things.

Jews Mock Yehoshua

Matt 27:39 But the passers-by reviled him, shaking their head,

40 and saying, Thou that destroy the temple and build it in three days, save thyself. If you are Son of the God, descend from the cross.

41 [And] in like manner the chief priests also, mocking, with the scribes and elders, said,

42 He saved others, himself he cannot save. He is King of Israel: let him descend now from the cross, and we will believe on him.

43 He trusted upon the God; let him save him now if he will [have] him. For he said, I am Son of God.

44 And the robbers also who had been crucified with him cast the same reproaches on him.

Luke 23:35 And the people stood beholding, and the rulers also [with them] sneered, saying, He has saved others; let him save himself if this is the Masiah, the chosen one of the God.

36 And the soldiers also made game of him, coming up offering him vinegar,

37 and saying, If you be the king of the Jews, save yourself.

Thief Next to Yehoshua Asks Remembrance

Luke 23:39 Now one of the malefactors who had been hung [on the cross] spoke insultingly to him, saying, Are not you the Masiah? save yourself and us.

40 But the other answering rebuked him, saying, Do you too not fear the God, you that are under the same judgment?

41 and we indeed justly, for we receive the just recompense of what we have done; but this [man] has done nothing amiss.

42 And he said to Yehoshua, Remember me, [lord] when you come in your kingdom.

43 And Yehoshua said to him, Truly I say to you today, "you shall be with me in paradise."

Yehoshua Asks John to Care for His Mother

John 19:25 And by the cross of Yehoshua stood his mother, and the sister of his mother, Mary the [wife] of Clopas, and Mary of Magdalene.

26 Yehoshua therefore, seeing his mother, and the disciple standing by, whom he loved, says to his mother, Woman, behold your son.

27 Then he says unto the disciple, Behold your mother. And from that hour the disciple took her to his own home.

Darkness between 12 noon and 3 P.M.

Last Moments on Cross

Matt 27:45 Now from the sixth hour [Jewish time or 12 noon] there was darkness over the whole land until the ninth hour [Jewish time or 3 p.m.],

46 but about the ninth hour Yehoshua cried out with a loud voice, saying, Eli, Eli, lama sabachthani? that is, My God, my God, why hast you forsaken me?

47 And some of those who stood there, when they heard it, said, This [man] calls for Elijah.

49 But the rest said, Let be; let us see if Elijah comes to save him.

John 19:28 After this, Yehoshua, knowing that all things were now finished, that the scripture might be fulfilled, says, I thirst.

29 There was a vessel therefore there full of vinegar, and having filled a sponge with vinegar, and putting hyssop round it, they put it up to his mouth.

Yehoshua Dies

30 When therefore Yehoshua had received the vinegar, he said, It is finished; and having bowed his head, he delivered up his spirit.

Luke 23:46 And Yehoshua, having cried with a loud voice, said, Father, into your hands I commit my spirit. And having said this, he expired.

Matt 27: 55 And there were there many women beholding from afar off, who had followed Yehoshua from Galilee ministering to him,

56 among whom was Mary of Magdala, and Mary the mother of James and Joses, and the mother of the sons of Zebedee.

Mark 15:39 And the centurion who stood by over against him, when he saw that he had expired having thus cried out, said, Truly this man was Son of God.

40 And there were women also looking on from afar off, among whom were both Mary of Magdalene, and Mary the mother of James the less and of Joses, and Salome;

41 who also, when he was in Galilee, followed him and ministered to him; and many others who came up with him to Jerusalem.

Luke 23:47 Now the centurion, seeing what took place, glorified the God, saying, In very deed this man was just.

48 And all the crowds who had come together to that sight, having seen the things that took place, returned, beating [their] breasts.

49 And all those who knew him stood afar off, the women also who had followed him from Galilee, beholding these things.

Preparation Day: Yehoshua is Pierced

John 19:31 The Jews therefore, that the bodies might not remain on the cross on the Sabbath, for it was the preparation, for the day of that Sabbath was a great [day] demanded of Pilate that their legs might be broken and they taken away.

32 The soldiers therefore came and broke the legs of the first and of the other that had been crucified with him;

33 but coming to Yehoshua, when they saw that he was already dead they did not break his legs,

34 but one of the soldiers pierced his side with a spear, and immediately there came out blood and water.

35 And he who saw it bears witness, and his witness is true, and he knows that he says true that you also may believe.

36 For these things took place that the scripture might be fulfilled,

> Not a bone of him shall be broken.

37 And again another scripture says,

> They shall look on him whom they pierced.

Joseph Asks for Body

Mark 15:42 And when it was already evening [before sunset], since it was the preparation, that is, [the day] before a Sabbath,

43 Joseph of Arimathaea, an honorable councillor, who also himself was awaiting the kingdom of the God, coming, emboldened himself and went in to Pilate and begged the body of Yehoshua.

44 And Pilate wondered if he were already dead; and having called to him the centurion, he inquired of him if he had long died.

45 And when he knew from the centurion, he granted the body to Joseph.

Yehoshua Buried

John 19:38 And after these things Joseph of Arimathaea, who was a disciple of Yehoshua, but secretly through fear of the Jews, asked of Pilate that he might take the body of Yehoshua: and Pilate allowed it. He came therefore and took away the body of Yehoshua.

39 And Nicodemus also, who at first came to Yehoshua by night, came, bringing a mixture of myrrh and aloes, about a hundred pounds [weight]

40 They took therefore the body of Yehoshua and bound it up in linen with the spices, as it is the custom with the Jews to prepare for burial.

41 But there was in the place where he had been crucified a garden, and in the garden a new tomb in which no one had ever been laid.

42 There therefore, on account of the preparation of the Jews, because the tomb was near, they laid Yehoshua.

Matt 27:59 And Joseph having got the body, wrapped it in a clean linen cloth,

60 and laid it in his new tomb which he had hewn in the rock; and having rolled a great stone to the door of the tomb, went away.

Masiah's Burial and Resurrection

The Biblical scriptures concerning Masiah's death were written by four: Matthew, Mark, Luke, and John. They each only wrote just part of the story. In order to understand all that went on at the time of Masiah's death; we must put all the scriptures together; we must collate them.

Three Days and Three Nights									
Wednesday		Thursday		Friday		Saturday		Sunday	
24 hour day		24 hour day		24 hour day		24 hour day		24 hour day	
night	day	night	day	night	day	night	day	night	day
14 Nisan Preparation day for the Passover		Passover an annual Sabbath				Sabbath a weekly Sabbath			
Buried just before or at sunset >		First Day		Second Day		Third Day Resurrected just before or at sunset>		Masiah (sheaf of first-fruits - Lev 23:9-14 Ascension to his Father near sunrise	
Resurrected after three full days (72 hours) in the grave at the very end of the 3rd day, just before the 4th day of the count									

In order to fulfill all these scriptures (A) & (B):

(1) According to Matt 12:40; John 2:19, 21, Jesus *must* have been resurrected in three days and nights after he was placed in the grave.

(2) According to point (1) and with Matt 16:21; 17:23; and Luke 9:22, Jesus *must* have been resurrected near the end of the third day (1= Thur.; 2= Fri.; 3=Saturday — the Sabbath).

(3) According to points (1) and (2) and with Mark 8:31 and 9:31, Jesus *must* have been resurrected three days after His death towards the very beginning of the fourth day (Sunday — first day of the new week).

Therefore in order to fulfill the very word of Christ about his burial for the three days and nights, and to fulfill the scriptures of the account of Jesus's death, burial, and resurrection, Jesus would have to have been buried[29] Wednesday before sunset, and he would have to be resurrected right after/at the three days and three nights later near the last part of Saturday (see Collation of Scriptures below). And scripture does indicate that Jesus died near the end of Wednesday (4th day of the week), was buried before sunset, and was in the grave three days (5th, 6th, & 7th day).

---

[29] Stone closing the tomb

Christ's Ascension

It was only the angel of the Lord who came (Matt 28:2). One angel came to the tomb. This is important, very important, for the women saw visions of two angels (John 20:12) or two men (Luke 24:4) or one young man (Mark 16:5) or one angel (Matt 28:5). Now we see that *one* angel came out of heaven to resurrect Christ the dead *man* (Matt 28:2). From here let's see how and when Jesus ascended to his Father.

Two Men; Two Angels?

The next morning after 7th day Sabbath, the women (Mary Magdalene; Mary; Joanna; and other women, John 20:l; Luke 24:9-10) came to the tomb and saw **two men**, according to Luke 24:4; or **an angel** according to Matthew 28:5; or **a young man** according to Mark 16:5. (See Robertson's Harmony of the Gospel, or our notes.) In Luke's account it says the two men spoke ("they said"). In the Matthew account it says the angel spoke. In the Mark account it says a young man spoke (Mark 16:6). Each of these renditions have the two men, the angel, and the young man, saying about the same thing. Surely this proves the Bible contradicts itself? Absolutely not!

Notice in Luke 24:5, "*they* said." Two spoke, for just before (V. 4), Luke said there were two men in the tomb. In Mark it says a young man was on the *right*, on the right there was a young man. Who was next to this young man? It was the angel (who looked like a man) who was next to the young man (Matt 28:5). Who came to resurrect Christ? It was the angel of the Lord (Matt 28:2-4). As we have shown you before (*God Papers* [GP3]) the angel of the Lord could either manifest himself as looking like a man, or like a flaming-fire. When he came to resurrect Christ, he came *looking* like a man. Thus, the young man (Christ) was on the right of the two who looked like men, and both spoke at once. There is no contradiction here. The scripture says merely that there were two who both looked like men, but one was a young man (Christ), and the other "man" was the angel of the Lord, who looked like a man.

After this event, the women went to the disciples (Luke 24:9-11; John 20:2; Luke 24:22-24) to tell them what had happened. With Peter and another disciple the women went back to the tomb that very Sunday morning. But on reaching the tomb they found nothing, but some linen cloths of Christ (John 20:6-7; Luke 24:12). Then the two disciples returned to the house of the disciples where they were meeting (John 20:10). But Mary Magdalene tarried behind, she was crying outside the tomb. Then she looked inside and saw two angels, according to John 20:11-13.

Now notice the two disciples had examined the tomb and did not see the two "men" that the women had seen, but they did see Christ's body was gone (Luke 24:22-24; John 20:6-9). Then these disciples left the tomb and headed back to the house again, but Mary stayed behind crying outside the tomb. Next she looked in and saw two angels. But the texts about the resurrection say only *one* angel came to resurrect Christ. Notice they were clothed in white. But so was the young man clothed in a white robe (Mark 16:5). Thus, as Luke called the angel of the Lord (Matt 28:5) and the resurrected Christ (Mark 16:5) two "men," so also did John call Christ and the angel of the Lord, two "angels." These two looked like men, but with their bright or white robes they also looked like angels. What do angels look like? They looked like burning flames (Heb 1:7; Acts 7:30). The bright, white light of their robes made them look like fire, thus, they looked like angels, and like men.

Mary, after the "angels" spoke to her, turned around "and beholds [that] the Jesus *had* stood, and she not known it was Jesus [standing as one of the two angels]" (John 20:14). Examine the King James Version, it implies she turned around and *then* saw Jesus. This is wrong. For in Greek the word translated "standing" and the words "knew not" are: one, a perfect tense participle, and two, a pluperfect tense verb in the indicative mood (in the 3rd person). Perfect tense words in Greek indicate *past* or *complete* action. Jesus was not standing after she turned, he *had* stood there before she turned. In other words, Jesus *had* stood with the angel of the Lord (as two "angels"), but Mary did not comprehend it. Further, a pluperfect tense word ("knew not" KJV) indicates a "*past state* resulting from *previous action*" (*Exegetical Grammar*, by J. Harold Greenlee, Eerdmans Pub, 1963). What was the previous action? It was the act of Mary turning. Thus, *before* this action Mary had seen Jesus, but "knew not" it was Jesus.

Fine. Mary had turned away from the two "angels" (one being Jesus, but she realized it not), and "Jesus says to her, why ... she supposing him to be the gardener" (John 20:15). She had turned away from the two "angels," then Jesus spoke to her, but she only thought it was a gardener. She must have been upset; this was an emotional evening, they didn't realize Christ was to be resurrected. They thought someone had stolen the body (V. 13). Mary had just seen two "angels" and talked to them. She turns away still crying and Jesus (now behind her, for she had turned away) spoke to her, but she believed it was a gardener. By the unbelievable events and her tears, one must conclude that she was somewhat upset. Now what?

Ascension & Fulfillment of Sheaf of the First Fruits

"Jesus said unto her [from behind], Mary. She turned herself [she turned now back to Jesus], and said to him, Rabboni, which is to say, Master. Jesus said unto her, *Touch me not*; for I am not yet ascended to my Father: but go to the brethren, and say unto them, I ascend unto my Father, and your Father; and to my God, and your God."(John 20:16-17)

Notice, Jesus would not let Mary touch him, for he hadn't ascended yet to his Father. Now notice *when* he ascended. "And behold! Jesus met them, saying, All hail. And they came and took hold of his feet, and worshiped him" (Matt 28:9). Who took hold of Christ's feet? — the women leaving the tomb, the *second* time. Remember these women went to the tomb in the morning at sunrise, and saw two "men." They went to the disciples and told them of it. The disciples rushed to the tomb. On seeing nothing they returned to their house. While they (the two disciples) returned, Mary tarried crying and Christ the resurrected man appeared to her. Then Mary went to tell the disciples about seeing Christ (John 20:18; Mark 16:10). Through a little comparison, we can see that Matthew 28:9-10 is Mary and the women returning home the *second* time from the tomb (see scripture below).

Right after Mary had spoken to Christ, Jesus ascended, for as they (Mary and the women, Matt 28:9-10) were returning Christ appeared to them again. But this time he allowed them to touch him. Yet what was his excuse for not allowing Mary to touch him (John 20:17)? — he hadn't yet ascended to his Father. Thus, because seconds or minutes later he did allow Mary and the other women to touch him, he *must* have ascended to his Father. This ascension of Christ fulfilled Spiritually

Lev 23:9-14, which occurs on a Sunday, the morrow after the Sabbath:

> Lev 23:9 Then the LORD spoke to Moses, saying, 10 "Speak to the sons of Israel and say to them, 'When you enter the land which I am going to give to you and reap its harvest, then you shall bring in **the sheaf of the first fruits of your harvest** to the priest. 11 'He shall wave the sheaf before the LORD for you to be accepted; **on the day <u>after</u> the Sabbath the priest shall wave it.**

Read "Sheaf of the First Fruits" in the NM 16, "God's Appointed Times," for more information on the sheaf of first fruits.

Also see *Prophecy Papers* 7 [PP7] under "Sheaf of the First Fruits," and *New Chronology Papers* 4 [CP4] under "Christ's Ascension."

Collation of Scriptures Pertaining to Christ's Burial and Resurrection

The Biblical scriptures concerning Christ's death were written by four: Matthew, Mark, Luke, and John. They each only wrote just part of the story. In order to understand all that went on at the time of Christ's death; we must put all the scriptures together; we must collate them. The following collation shows Christ's pre-death words were true, he would be in the grave for three full days and nights. The scriptures quoted below are from the BCB translation unless otherwise stated.

Comments	Scripture	Matt	Mark	Luke	John
Wednesday, 14th of Nisan Christ died on the day of Preparation as the day drew on towards the first annual Sabbath (High day -- John 19:31) of the Passover festival. The True Passover (Christ) was killed on the 14th day of the first month of the Hebrew's Calendar (Ex 12:6; Num 28:16).	Lk 23:54 And it was preparation day, and [the] Sabbath was coming on. Lk 23:55 And women, who had come along with him out of Galilee, having followed, saw the tomb and how his body was placed.			23:54-55	
Thursday, 15th of Nisan; _First Day_ The first annual Sabbath of the Passover after Christ died was Thursday the 15th of Nisan on the Hebrew or Jewish Calendar (Num 28:17-18).	This being the Sabbath (an annual Sabbath) spoken about in Luke 23:54.			23:54 ("Sab. drew near")	

Comments	Scripture	Matt	Mark	Luke	John
Friday, 16th of Nisan; _Second Day_ After the **annual Sabbath** on the 15th of Nisan, the women buy spices and prepare them for Christ's body on the day _after_ the annual Sabbath, for no Jew was allowed to buy such items on a Sabbath (Neh 10:31). This Sabbath was a High day of the festival, not the weekly Sabbath.	Mark 16:1 And the [first] Sabbath being [now] past, Mary of Magdalene, and Mary the [mother] of James, and Salome, bought aromatic spices that they might come and embalm him. Lk 23:56 And having returned they prepared aromatic spices and ointments,		16:1	23:56 a	
Saturday, 17th of Nisan, a weekly Sabbath day ; _The Third Day_ The women rest on the regular weekly Sabbath	Lk 23:56b and rested on the Sabbath[7th day], according to the commandment.			23:56 b	
After **the 7th day Sabbath, 18th of Nisan** on Sunday morning, the women begin to travel to the tomb with the spices for the body of Christ.	Mat 28:1 Now after the [two] Sabbaths [of the two Sabbaths in the Passover week] it being Sunday morning, towards first of the [next 2] Sabbaths [in the next week], came Mary the Magdala and the other Mary to look at the tomb	28:1			
The angel of the Lord resurrects Christ on the 3rd day after his death. This scripture describes the resurrection that happened at the end of the 7th day Sabbath on the **17th of Nisan**.	Mat 28: 2 And behold, there was a **great earthquake**; for an angel of [the] Lord, descending out of heaven, came and rolled away the stone and sat upon it 3 And his look was as lightning, and his clothing white as snow 4 And for fear of him the guards trembled and became as dead men **Note**: The resurrection of the dead saints and the dividing of the door [or veil] to the holy of holies occurred with the resurrection of Christ at the end of the 7th day Sabbath when the **earthquake** happened. (Matt 27:51-54) There was only one earthquake.	28:2-4			

Comments	Scripture	Matt	Mark	Luke	John
On Sunday, 18th of Nisan, in morning before or at sunrise the women come to the tomb.	John 20:1a And in first [day] of the [next week of] Sabbaths Mary of Magdalene comes early morning (darkness yet taken place) to the tomb, Mark 16:2 And very early morning in the [next week of] Sabbaths they come to the tomb, the sun having risen. 3 And they said to one another, Who shall roll us away the stone out of the door of the tomb? Lk 24:1 But in first [day of the next week] of the Sabbaths very early indeed in the morning, they came to the tomb, bringing the aromatic spices which they had prepared.		16:2-3	24:1	20:1a
Sunday, 18th Nisan On reaching the tomb, they see the stone in front of the tomb was moved.	Mark 16:4 And when they looked, they see that the stone has been rolled [away] for it was very great. Lk 24:2 And they found the stone rolled away from the tomb. John 20:1b and sees the stone taken away from the tomb.		16:4	24:2	20:1b
They then enter the tomb; the body is gone.	Lk 24:3 And when they had entered they found not the body of the Lord Jesus. Mark 16:5a And entering into the tomb,		16:5a	24:3	
Sunday, early in the morning. BUT they see two "men" (one angel [Matt 28:5] and one man [Mark 16:5]; both looked like they were either an angel or a man in bright-white clothes, see CP4).	Lk 24:4 And it came to pass as they were in perplexity about it, that behold, two men suddenly stood by them in shining raiment.			24:4	

Comments	Scripture	Matt	Mark	Luke	John
One of these two was a young man on the right.	Mark 16:5 And entering into the tomb, they saw a young man sitting on the right, clothed in a white robe, and they were amazed and alarmed;		16:5		
The two "men" said, "Why seek ..."	Lk 24:5 And as they were filled with fear and bowed their faces to the ground, they said to them, Why seek you the living one among the dead?			24:5	
The "angel," "he," "they" continue to speak	Mat 28:5 And the angel answering said to the women, Fear not, for I know that you seek Jesus the crucified one 6 He is not here, for he is risen, as he said. Come, see the place where the Lord lay 7 And go quickly and say to his disciples that he is risen from the dead; and behold, he goes before you into Galilee, there shall you see him. Behold, I have told you Mark 16:6 but he says to them, Be not alarmed. You seek Jesus, the Nazarene, the crucified one. He is risen, he is not here; behold the place where they had put him. 7 But go, tell his disciples and Peter, he goes before you into Galilee; there shall you see him, as he said to you. Lk 24:6 He is not here, but is risen: remember how he spoke to you, being yet in Galilee, 7 saying, The Son of man must be delivered up into the hands of sinners, and be crucified, and rise the third day. 8 And they remembered his words;	28:5-7	16:6-7	24:6-8	

Comments	Scripture	Matt	Mark	Luke	John
The women flee the tomb astonished	Mat 28:8 And going out quickly from the tomb with fear and great joy, they ran to bring his disciples word Mark 16:8 And they went out, and fled from the tomb. And trembling and excessive amazement possessed them, and they said nothing to any one, for they were afraid.	28:8	16:8		
The women speak about what they saw to the disciples	Lk 24:9 and, returning from the tomb, related all these things to the eleven and to all the rest. 10 Now it was Mary of Magdalene, and Johanna, and Mary the [mother] of James, and the others with them, who told these things to the apostles. John 20:2 She runs therefore and comes to Simon Peter, and to the other disciple, to whom Jesus was attached, and says to them, They have taken away the Lord out of the tomb, and we know not where they have laid him.			24:9-10	20:2
Their words seemed as foolish talk to the disciples	Lk 24:11 And their words appeared in their eyes as an idle tale, and they disbelieved them.			24:11	
Yet Peter went with the women back to the tomb, but another disciple outran Peter to the tomb; both saw that the body of Christ was gone. They departed wondering, for they didn't understand that Christ must first suffer then be resurrected after three days.	Lk 24:12 But Peter, rising up, ran to the tomb, and stooping down he sees the linen clothes lying there alone, and went away home, wondering at what had happened. John 20:3 Peter therefore went forth, and the other disciple, and came to the tomb. 4 And the two ran together, and the other disciple ran forward faster than Peter, and came first to the tomb, 5 and stooping down he sees the linen cloths lying; he did not however go in. 6 Simon Peter therefore comes, following him, and entered into the tomb, and sees the linen cloths lying, 7 and the towel which was upon his head, not lying with the linen cloths, but folded up in a distinct place by itself. 8 Then entered in therefore the other disciple also who came first to the tomb, and he saw and believed; 9 for they had not yet known the			24:12	20:3-10

Comments	Scripture	Matt	Mark	Luke	John
	scripture, that he must rise from among [the] dead. 10 The disciples therefore went away again to their own home.				
BUT Mary Magdalene and others (John 20:1 & Matt 28:1) tarried behind; Jesus then appeared to Mary (but Jesus said she couldn't touch him until he ascended to his Father).	Mark 16:9 Now when he had risen, very early towards the first [day] of the week, he appeared first to Mary of Magdalene, out of whom he had cast seven daemons. John 20:11 But Mary stood at the tomb weeping outside. As therefore she wept, she stooped down into the tomb, 12 and beholds two angels sitting in white [garments] one at the head and one at the feet, where the body of Jesus had lain. 13 And they say to her, Woman, why do you weep? She says to them, Because they have taken away my Lord, and I know not where they have laid him. 14 Having said these things she turned backward and beholds Jesus standing [there] and knew not that it was Jesus. 15 Jesus says to her, Woman, why do you weep? Whom do you seek? She, supposing that it was the gardener, says to him, Sir, if you have borne him hence, tell me where you have laid him, and I will take him away. 16 Jesus says to her, Mary. She, turning round, says to him in Hebrew, Rabboni, which means Teacher. 17 Jesus says to her, Touch me not, for I have not yet ascended towards my Father; but go to my brethren and say to them, I ascend towards the Father of me and Father of you, and [to] my God and your God.		16:9		20:11-17
Moments later Jesus appeared to the women (Mary Magdalene and the others who tarried with her) as they were going back from the tomb to the disciples the second time (this time Jesus allows them to touch him,	Mat 28:9 And as they went to bring his disciples word, behold also, Jesus met them, saying, Hail! And they coming up took him by the feet, and did him homage. 10 Then Jesus says to them, Fear not; go, bring word to my brethren that they go into Galilee, and there they shall see me.	28:9-10			

Comments	Scripture	Matt	Mark	Luke	John
thus, he in this short time had ascended to his Father).					
Sunday, after Sabbath sunset While the women continue to the disciples, the guards tell the chief priests a lie when they were explaining what had occurred (see, Matt 28:2-4). Please read these verse to see what they said and how they lied.	Mat 28:11 And as they went, behold, some of the watch went into the city, and brought word to the chief priests of all that had taken place. 12 And having assembled with the elders, and having taken counsel, they gave a large sum of money to the soldiers, 13 saying, Say that his disciples coming by night stole him [while] we [were] sleeping. 14 And if this should come to the hearing of the governor, we will persuade him, and save you from all anxiety. 15 And they took the money and did as they had been taught. And this report is current among the Jews until this day.	28:1 1- 15			
The women (Matt 28:8,9,11) continue to the house where the disciples were staying at. Mary tells the disciples that they saw Jesus and they held him and they relate what He said, but the disciples didn't believe.	Mark 16:10 She went and brought word to those that had been with him, [who were] grieving and weeping. 11 And when these heard that he was alive and had been seen of her, they disbelieved [it]. John 20:18 Mary of Magdalene comes bringing word to the disciples that she had seen the Lord, and [that] he had said these things to her.		16:10 - 11		20:18
Sunday, during the day light and before sunset Christ manifests Himself in another form (different from Mark 16:9 & John 20:17; but probably like Matt 28:9 & Luke 24:39) to two disciples going to a village of Emmaus. On reaching it they perceived it was Christ who was walking and talking	Mark 16:12 And after these things he was manifested in another form to two of them as they walked, going into the country; 13 and they went and brought word to the rest; neither did they believe them. Lk 24:13 And behold, two of them were going on that same day [Sunday] to a village distant sixty stadia [few miles] from Jerusalem, called Emmaus; 14 and they conversed with one another about all these things which had taken place. 15 And it came to pass as they		16:12 - 13	24:13- 32	

Comments	Scripture	Matt	Mark	Luke	John
with them. Then Christ vanished out of sight.	conversed and reasoned, that Jesus himself drawing near, went with them; 16 but their eyes were holden so as not to know him. 17 And he said to them, What discourses are these which pass between you as you walk, and are downcast? 18 And one [of them] named Cleopas, answering said to him, Are you alone sojourning in Jerusalem, and do not know what has taken place in it in these days? 19 And he said to them, What things? And they said to him, The things concerning Jesus the Nazarene, who was a prophet mighty in deed and word before the God and all the people; 20 and how the chief priests and our rulers delivered him up to [the] judgment of death and crucified him. 21 But we had hoped that he was [the one] who is about to redeem Israel. Yes, and along with all this, this brings on *the* third day since these things [v. 20] took place. 22 And certain women from among us astonished us, having been very early at the tomb [on this third day], [The women went to the tomb at the very end of the third reaching the tomb right after Jesus was resurrected on the very beginning of the fourth day, that is, the first day of the new week. See *New Chronology Papers*, Part 4] 23 and, not having found his body [right after sunset on the fourth day], came, saying that they also had seen a vision of angels, who say that he is living. 24 And some of those with us went to the tomb, and found it so, as the women also had said, but him they saw not. 25 And he [Jesus] said to them, O senseless and slow of heart to believe in all that the prophets have spoken! 26 Ought not the Christ to have suffered these things and to enter into his glory? 27 And having begun from Moses and from all the prophets, he interpreted to them in all the scriptures the things concerning himself.				

Comments	Scripture	Matt	Mark	Luke	John
	28 And they drew near to the village where they were going, and he made as though he would go farther. 29 And they constrained him, saying, Stay with us, for it is toward evening and the day is declining. And he entered in to stay with them. 30 And it came to pass as he was at table with them, having taken the bread, he blessed, and having broken it, gave it to them. 31 And their eyes were opened, and they recognized him. And he disappeared from them. 32 And they said to one another, Was not our heart burning in us as he spoke to us on the way, [and] as he opened the scriptures to us?				
After this, the two who were going to the village, returned to Jerusalem and grouped with the disciples, and told the disciples that Jesus appeared to them (the two being Simon and Cleopas (Luke 24:18, 34).	Mark 16:14a Afterwards as they lay at table he was manifested to the eleven, Lk 24:33 And rising up the same hour, they returned to Jerusalem. And they found the eleven, and those with them, gathered together, 34 saying, The Lord is indeed risen and has appeared to Simon. 35 And they related what [had happened] on the way, and how he was made known to them in the breaking of bread. 1CO 15:5 KJV And that he was seen of Cephas,		16:14 a	24:33-35	
At this time, Christ manifested Himself to eleven disciples, but without Thomas (Luke 24:33; John 20:24).	Mark 16:14 Afterwards as they lay at table he was manifested to the eleven, and reproached [them with] their unbelief and hardness of heart, because they had not believed those who had seen him risen.		16:14		20:19

Comments	Scripture	Matt	Mark	Luke	John
	John 20:19 When therefore it was evening on that day, which was first [day] of the week, and the doors shut where the disciples were, through fear of the Jews, Jesus came and stood in the midst, and says to them, Peace [be] to you.				
The disciples feared this appearance of Christ who seemed to come from nowhere -- they thought He was a spirit.	Lk 24:36 And as they were saying these things, he himself stood in their midst, and says to them, Peace [be] unto you. 37 But they, being confounded and being frightened, supposed they beheld a spirit.			24:36-37	
Jesus questioned their unbelief	Mark 16:14b and reproached [them with] their unbelief and hardness of heart, because they had not believed those who had seen him risen. Lk 24:38 And he said to them, Why are you troubled? and why are thoughts rising in your hearts?		16:14 b	24:38	
Christ shows the disciples He is flesh and blood	Lk 24:39 behold my hands and my feet, that it is I myself. Handle me and see, for a spirit has not flesh and bones as you see me having. 40 And having said this he showed them his hands and his feet. John 20:20 And having said this, he showed to them his hands and his side. The disciples rejoiced therefore, having seen the Lord.			24:39-40	20:20
He eats with them also	Lk 24:41 But while they yet did not believe for joy, and were wondering, he said to them, Have you anything here to eat? 42 And they gave him part of a broiled fish and of a honeycomb; 43 and he took it and ate before them.			24:41-43	
Jesus Christ explains scripture about His death and gives a commission; Thomas is not with	Lk 24:44 And he said to them, These [are] the words which I spoke to you while I was yet with you, that all that is written concerning me in the law of Moses and prophets and psalms must be fulfilled.			24:44-49	20:21-25

Comments	Scripture	Matt	Mark	Luke	John
them, and Thomas doesn't believe Christ appeared.	45 Then he opened their understanding to understand the scriptures,				
	46 and said to them, Thus it is written, and thus it behooved the Christ to suffer, and to rise from among the dead the third day;				
	47 and that repentance and forgiveness of sins should be preached in his name to all the nations beginning at Jerusalem.				
	48 And you are witnesses of these things.				
	49 And behold, I send the promise of my Father upon you; but do you remain in the city till you be clothed with power from on high.				
	John 20:21 [Jesus] said therefore again to them, Peace [be] to you: as the Father sent me forth, I also send you.				
	22 And having said this, he breathed into [them] and says to them, Receive [the] Holy Spirit:				
	23 whose sins you remit, they are remitted to them; whose sins you retain, they are retained.				
	24 But Thomas, one of the twelve, called Didymus, was not with them when Jesus came.				
	25 The other disciples therefore said to him, We have seen the Lord. But he said to them, Unless I see in his hands the mark of the nails, and put my finger into the mark of the nails, and put my hand into his side, I will not believe.				
	ACT 1:4a KJV And, being assembled together with them, commanded them that they should not depart from Jerusalem, but wait for the promise of the Father ...				
	5 For John truly baptized with water; but ye shall be baptized with the Holy Ghost not many days hence.				
Eight Days Later Jesus appears eight days later to the 12 disciples; Thomas sees Christ and believes -- calls Him his	John 20:26 And eight days after, his disciples were again within, and Thomas with them. Jesus comes, the doors being shut, and stood in the midst and said, Peace [be] to you.				20:26-31
	27 Then he says to Thomas, Bring your finger here and see my hands; and bring				

Comments	Scripture	Matt	Mark	Luke	John
Lord and his God.	your hand and put it into my side; and be not unbelieving, but believing. 28 Thomas answered and said to him, The Lord of me and the God of me. 29 Jesus says to him, Because you have seen me you have believed: blessed they who have not seen and have believed. 30 Many other signs therefore also Jesus did before his disciples, which are not written in this book; 31 but these are written that you may believe that Jesus is the Christ, the Son of the God, and that believing you might have life in his name.				
Thereafter Christ later appeared again near the sea of Galilee (Tiberias) as he said he would appear to all the brethren (Mark 16:7; Matt 28:7;Luke 24:6-7; Matt 28:9-10; etc.)	John 21:1 After these things Jesus manifested himself again to the disciples at the sea of Tiberias. And he manifested [himself] thus. 2 There were together Simon Peter, and Thomas called Didymus, and Nathanael who was of Cana of Galilee, and the [sons] of Zebedee, and two others of his disciples. 3 Simon Peter says to them, I go to fish. They say to him, We also come with you. They went forth, and went on board, and that night took nothing. 4 And early morn already breaking, Jesus stood on the shore; the disciples however did not know that it was Jesus. 5 Jesus therefore says to them, Children, have you anything to eat? They answered him, No. 6 And he said to them, Cast the net at the right side of the ship and you will find. They cast therefore, and they could no longer draw it, from the multitude of fishes. 7 That disciple therefore whom Jesus loved says to Peter, It is the Lord. Simon Peter therefore, having heard that it was the Lord, girded his overcoat [on him] for he was naked, and cast himself into the sea; 8 and the other disciples came in the small boat, for they were not far from the land, but somewhere about two hundred cubits, dragging the net of fishes.				21:1-23

Comments	Scripture	Matt	Mark	Luke	John
	9 When therefore they went out on the land, they see a fire of coals there, and fish laid on it, and bread.				
	10 Jesus says to them, Bring of the fishes which you have now taken.				
	11 Simon Peter went up and drew the net to the land full of great fishes, a hundred and fifty-three; and though there were so many, the net was not rent.				
	12 Jesus says to them, Come [and] dine. But none of the disciples dared inquire of him, Who are you? knowing that it was the Lord.				
	13 Jesus comes and takes the bread and gives it to them, and the fish in like manner.				
	14 This is already the third time that Jesus had been manifested to the disciples, being risen from among [the] dead.				
	15 When therefore they had dined, Jesus says to Simon Peter, Simon, [son] of Jonas, do you love me more than these? He says to him, Yes, Lord; you know that I am attached to you. He says to him, Feed my lambs.				
	16 He says to him again a second time, Simon, [son] of Jonas, do you love you me? He says to him, Yes, Lord; you know that I am attached to you. He says to him, Shepherd my sheep.				
	17 He says to him the third time, Simon, [son] of Jonas, are you attached to me? Peter was grieved because he said to him the third time, Are you attached to me? and said to him, Lord, you know all things; you know that I am attached to you. Jesus says to him, Feed my sheep.				
	18 Truly, truly, I say to you, When you were young, you girded yourself, and walked where you desired; but when you shall be old, you shall stretch forth your hands, and another shall gird you, and bring you where you do not desire.				
	19 But he said this signifying by what death he should glorify the God. And having said this, he says to him, Follow me.				
	20 Peter, turning round, sees the				

Comments	Scripture	Matt	Mark	Luke	John
	disciple whom Jesus loved following, who also leaned at supper on his breast, and said, Lord, who is it that delivers you up? 21 Peter, seeing him, says to Jesus, Lord, and what [of] this [man] 22 Jesus says to him, If I wish that he abide until I come, what [is that] to you? You follow me. 23 This word therefore went out among the brethren, That disciple does not die. And Jesus did not say to him, He does not die; but, If I wish that he abide until I come, what [is that] to you?				
Christ at this same time appeared in Galilee to 500 as he promised.	1CO 15:6 KJV After that, he was seen of above five hundred brethren at once; of whom the greater part remain unto this present, but some are fallen asleep.				
Christ then leads them over against Bethany into the appointed mountain.	Mat 28:16 But the eleven disciples went into Galilee to the mountain which Jesus had appointed them 17 And when they saw him, they did homage to him: but some doubted Lk 24:50 And he led them out as far as Bethany, and having lifted up his hands, he blessed them.	28:16-17		24:50	
Jesus in the mountain teaches that the knowledge of the end of the age was in his Father's hand.	ACT 1:6 KJV When they therefore were come together, they asked of him, saying, Lord, wilt thou at this time restore again the kingdom to Israel? 7 And he said unto them, It is not for you to know the times or the seasons, which the Father hath put in his own power.				
BUT he notes all power was given to Him. ["All things that the Father has are mine; therefore I said, that He shall take of mine, and shall show it unto you" (John 16:15).]	Mat 28:18 And Jesus coming up spoke to them, saying, All power has been given me in heaven and upon earth	28:18			
Jesus says they will receive the power of the Spirit.	ACT 1:8a KJV But ye shall receive power, after that the Holy Ghost is come upon you:				

Comments	Scripture	Matt	Mark	Luke	John
["Howbeit when he the Spirit of Truth, is come, he will guide you into all truth" (John 16:13)]					
He then tells them to preach the gospel to ALL and baptize "them into the NAME of the Father, and of the Son, and of the Holy Spirit."	Mat 28:19 Go [therefore] and make disciples of all the nations, baptizing them into the name of the Father, and of the Son, and of the Holy Spirit 20 teaching them to observe all things whatsoever I have enjoined you. And behold, I am with you all the days, until the completion of the age [aeon]. Mark 16:15 And he said to them, Go into all the world, and preach the good news to all the creation. ACT 1:8b KJV and ye shall be witnesses unto me both in Jerusalem, and in all Judaea, and in Samaria, and unto the uttermost part of the earth.	28:19-20	16:15		
Christ further gives them power	Mark 16:16 He that believes and is baptized shall be saved, and he that disbelieves shall be condemned. 17 And these signs shall follow those that have believed: in my name they shall cast out daemons; they shall speak with new tongues; 18 they shall take up serpents; and if they should drink any deadly thing it shall not injure them; they shall lay hands upon the infirm, and they shall be well.		16:16-18		
and he said He would be with the Church until the end of the age.	Mat 28:20b And behold, I am with you all the days, until the completion of the age [aeon].	28:20b			
After this commission was given to the apostles by Christ on the mountain, He then ascends into heaven.	Mark 16:19 The Lord therefore, after he had spoken to them, was taken up into heaven, and sat at the right hand of the God. Lk 24:51 And it came to pass as he was blessing them, he was separated from them and was carried up into heaven. ACT 1:9 KJV And when he had spoken these things, while they beheld, he was taken up; and a cloud received him out		16:19	24:51	

Comments	Scripture	Matt	Mark	Luke	John
	of their sight.				
But lo! two others were there.	ACT 1:10 KJV And while they looked stedfastly toward heaven as he went up, behold, two men stood by them in white apparel; 11 Which also said, Ye men of Galilee, why stand ye gazing up into heaven? this same Jesus, which is taken up from you into heaven, shall so come in like manner as ye have seen him go into heaven.				
A list of those on the hill is given.	ACT 1:13 KJV And when they were come in, they went up into an upper room, where abode both Peter, and James, and John, and Andrew, Philip, and Thomas, Bartholomew, and Matthew, James the son of Alphaeus, and Simon Zelotes, and Judas the brother of James. 14 These all continued with one accord in prayer and supplication, with the women, and Mary the mother of Jesus, and with his brethren.				
The disciples returned to Jerusalem from the appointed mountain.	Lk 24:52 And they, having done him homage, returned to Jerusalem with great joy, ACT 1:12 KJV Then returned they unto Jerusalem from the mount called Olivet, which is from Jerusalem a Sabbath day's journey.			24:52	
The disciples teach in the temple.	Mark 16:20 And they, going forth, preached everywhere, the Lord working with [them] and confirming the word by the signs following upon [it] Lk 24:53 and were continually in the temple praising and blessing the God.		16:20	24:53	

Passover Scriptures Reiteration

Passover Scriptures

gn1» The chief priests of the Jews had a meeting wherein they took counsel to kill Christ (John 11:47-53; Luke 22:2). Because of those out to kill him, Christ no more could walk openly. (John 11:54)

gn2» Now the passover wherein Christ was killed was near, and many had come to Jerusalem for the festival and were wondering among themselves whether Christ would show up at the festival. The chief priests had given direction that if any knew where Christ was that they should point him out to them so the priests could take Jesus. (John 11:55-57)

9th of Nisan, a Friday

gn3» Then six days before the passover (the 9th of Nisan), Christ came to Bethany which is only a few miles from Jerusalem. (John 12:1; 11:17)

At that time they had a supper wherein Mary anointed the feet of Jesus, and wiped his feet with her hair. (John 12:2-3; Mark 14:3; Matt 26:6-7)

Now some of the disciples had indignation inside their minds at this act, and one named Judas Iscariot, said: "Why was not this ointment sold for three hundred pence, and given to the poor?" (Mark 14:4-5; Matt 26:8-9; John 12:4-6)

Then when Jesus understood what was being said, he spoke saying, "let her alone: that of the day of my burial may she keep it" (John 12:7). The Mary that anointed Christ was Mary Magdalene, who later brought this ointment to Christ's tomb on the day of his resurrection along with some spices she and others had bought and prepared the day before Christ's resurrection (Luke 23:56-24:1; Mark 16:1; Matt 28:1). (John 12:7-8; Mark 14:6-9; Matt 26:10-13)

10th of Nisan, a Saturday

gn4» Now right after this supper, right after sunset, thus on the 10th of Nisan, Judas the betrayer of Christ went to the chief priests and said he would help them take Jesus in the absence of a great crowd. Because of this the priests were glad that Judas would betray Christ, and agreed to give him 30 pieces of silver. Further, they consulted if they shouldn't also put Lazarus to death since many of the Jews believed in Jesus because Christ had previously resurrected Lazarus from the dead. (Mark 14:10-11; Matt 26:14-16; Luke 22:3-6; John 12:9-11)

On the next day after Christ came to Bethany, which was the daylight hours of the same 24 hour day that Judas had agreed to betray Christ to the priests, Christ came into Jerusalem — 10th day of Nisan (John 12:12).

Christ rode on an ass into Jerusalem, and the people cried, "Hosanna; Blessed is he that comes in the name of the Lord." This was the 10th day of the Jews 1st month — Nisan. (Mark 11:1-10; Matt 21:1-11; Luke 19:28-40)

Now in the 10th day of Nisan after he entered into Jerusalem, Jesus went into the temple (Mark 11:11).

Then in the evening just before sunset, Christ went into Bethany, a town about two miles from Jerusalem. (Mark 11:11)

First Week with Two Sabbaths

11th of Nisan, a Sunday

gn5» Now in the morrow (the next day, that is the 11th of Nisan), Christ came from Bethany back into Jerusalem. (Mark 11:12-15)

Now it was the 11th, and again Christ goes into the temple in Jerusalem. (Mark 11:15; Luke 19:45; Matt 21:12)

At this time Christ put the money changers out of the temple (Matt 21:12-16; Mark 11:15-18; Luke 19:45-46).

During this time period just before the Passover, Christ was teaching daily in the temple. (Luke 19:47)

Then in the evening of the 11th he went out of Jerusalem again and went into Bethany. (Mark 11:19; Matt 21:17)

12th of Nisan, a Monday

gn6» After he stayed in Bethany, he came back into Jerusalem on the next day, the 12th. (Mark 11:20; Matt 21:18)

Now when they returned into Jerusalem, the disciples with Christ noticed the tree Christ cursed the previous day (Mark 11:13-14), and how it already had dried up (Mark 11:21; Matt 21:19-20).

At this time on the 12th Christ entered again into the temple (Matt 21:23; Mark 11:27; Luke 20:1).

At this time on the 12th, Christ taught various parables (Matt 21:23-23:39; Mark 11:27-12:44; Luke 20:1-21:4).

Then Christ went out of the temple, and taught his disciples on the mount of Olives about the time of the end of the age (Mark 13:1-33; Luke 21:5-36: Matt 24:1-25:46).

At that time on the 12th of Nisan, Christ noted that after two days would be the feast of unleavened bread, which some call the passover festival (Luke 22:1). (Matt 26:1-2; Mark 14:1)

At this time Christ mentioned that he is betrayed (for on the 10th remember Judas went to the chief priests to betray Jesus) (Matt 26:2).

The chief priests had decided at that time that Christ shouldn't be taken on the feast day (the 15th, Num 28:17), because there might be an uproar among the people. (Matt 26:3-5; Mark 14:1-2)

But remember on the 10th Judas had come to the chief priests, and said he would betray Jesus (John 12:1-11; Luke 22:3-6; Mark 14:3-11; Matt 26:6-16).

After Christ had returned from the temple on the 12th, after he taught many parables (see above), and after he on Mount Olives had spoken of the end of the age that late evening of the 12th (or early on the 13th after sunset), he then stayed on Mount Olives in Bethany (note Luke 24:50 with Acts 1:12). (Luke 21:37)

13th of Nisan, a Tuesday

gn7» The next day on the 13th, Jesus taught in the temple again after he abode in Bethany the night of the 13th, for at this time Jesus was teaching daily in the temple (Luke 19:47) (Luke 21:38).

Now before the feast of the passover, on the evening of the 13th, after Christ had taught during the daylight of the 13th in the temple, he was again in Bethany, and was eating his supper, as he had been doing each evening since he had began teaching in the temple on the 10th (John 13:1).

The home he was staying in was that of Mary Magdalene, Martha, and Lazarus (John 12:1).

Now Jesus on the 13th had instructed the apostles to get a room and make it ready for the passover meal, which was to occur on the 14th (Matt 26:17-19; Mark 14:12-16; Luke 22:7-13).

gn8» [[Let's correct a few verses that may be a mistranslated in many English translations of the Bible. These corrections were made by a Greek text.

Matt 26:17 should read: "now *towards* the first [day] of unleavened [bread] approaches the disciples to Jesus ..." And Mark 14:12 should read: "and *towards* the first day of the unleavened [bread], when they kill the passover, his disciples say to him....." And Luke 22:7 should read: "now it came *towards* the day of unleavened [bread], in which was needful to be killed the passover." Therefore what these verses are saying is that *towards* or near the 14th day when the passover was to be killed, the disciples had asked Christ where they would eat the passover the next day. Now in Matthew 26:19, Mark 14:16, and Luke 22:13 the Greek verbal word translated "they made ready" is an aorist word that indicates an action without indicating the time of the action. Thus, it can mean action in the past, present, or future. According to the context of this verse this Greek word should have been rendered in the following manner: "were to make ready" the passover in the certain house where Christ said to prepare it. Christ had ordered them to prepare for the passover, but the events surrounding Christ's betrayal made it impossible to go and eat the Passover.]]

gn9» Now the evening of the 13th came and Christ was in Bethany at supper with his disciples. "And supper taking place..." (John 13:2; Matt 26: 20-21; Mark 14:17-18; Luke 22:14).

gn10» Christ time after time taught the disciples that the greatest thing was to serve others (Luke 9:46-48; Mark 10:42-44). And again on the evening of the 13th he again by using the example of washing their feet, said that the greatest thing was to serve, not to lord over others. "It is more blessed to give then to receive" (Acts 20:35). The washing of the feet was a reiteration of the principle of giving and serving. We try our best to follow this principle always, not just on one day of the year.

gn11» Now during this meal Jesus broke the bread, and passed it around, and said he could "not eat it," the Passover, with them until it was fulfilled in the kingdom of God. (Luke 22:15-20; Mark 14:22-24; Matt 26:26-29)

gn12» And during this meal, Christ revealed who would deliver him up that night (14th, after sunset; after the supper they were eating on the 13th before sunset). (Matt 26:21-25; Mark 14:18-21; Luke 22:21-23; John 13:21-29)

14th of Nisan, a Wednesday

gn13»

(1) It was Judas Iscariot, and right after he took the piece of bread, which pointed him out as the betrayer (yet the apostles didn't understand), Judas immediately went out, "and it was night." That is, right after sunset Judas went out to bring the chief priests to take Jesus. (John 13:30) They were in Bethany, which is on the side of Mount Olives, when they were eating this meal (see above).

(2) After they sang a hymn, they went onto Mount Olives, and brought two swords with them so scripture could be fulfilled (Mark 14:26; Matt 26:30; Luke 22:35-39).

(3) On Mount Olives Christ speaks of various matters to the apostles. (The scripture is vague as to whether these things were spoke still in the house in Bethany, or near the house, or somewhere on the mount of Olives.) (Mark 14:26-31; Matt 26:31-35; John 13:31-17:36)

(4) At Gethsemane (probably on the mount of Olives) he enters into a garden to pray. (Matt 26:36-46; Mark 14:32-42; Luke 22:40-46; John 18:1)

(5) Now Judas knew where this garden was, for Jesus came often to it to pray (John 18:2).

(6) It was in this garden that Judas came with the chief priests and Pharisees, who came with lanterns and torches because it was at night on the 14th after sunset (John 18:3; Luke 22:47; Mark 14:43; Matt 26:47).

(7) At this time Judas revealed Christ by greeting him with a kiss. Peter cut off an ear of a guard, but Christ healed the ear. Then *all* the disciples "forsook him, and fled." (Matt 26:47-56; Mark 14:43-52; Luke 22:47-53; John 18:4-11)

(8) Then the band of men with the chief priests bound Christ and brought him, and let him away to Annas *first*, for he was the father-in-law to Caiaphas, who was the high priest that same year (John 18:12-13).

(9) Then they took Christ to Caiaphas the high priest (John 18:24).

(10) During that time Peter denied Christ three times as Jesus foretold (John 18:15-27; Luke 22:54-65; Mark 14:66-72; Matt 26:69-75). The cock crowed in early morning.

[Morning was come" (Matt 27:1; Mark 15:1); "and as it was morning, the elders of the people and the chief priests" (Luke 22:66). Or, "and it was morning; and they themselves went not into the judgment hall" (John 18:28)]

(11) In this morning part of the day, the chief priests and the elders came to take Christ, and right after they had him briefly before the high priest, they brought him to the judgement hall to Pilate (John 18:28-29; Luke 22:66-71; 23:1; Mark 15:1; Matt 27:1-2). Pilate sent Jesus to Herod Antipas because "he knew that he was of Herod's jurisdiction" (Luke 23:6-7). But Herod after mocking Jesus sent him back to Pilate (Luke 23:8-12).

(12) Then Jesus was tried and sent to be crucified (John 18:29-19:16; Luke 23:2-25; Mark 15:2-20; Matt 27:2-31).

(13) Now during that day Judas the Betrayer killed himself (Matt 27:3-10; Acts 1:16-20).

(14) Then they crucified Christ. (Matt 27:32-56; Mark 15:21-41; Luke 23:26-49; John 19:16-37)

(15) Now the Passover was prepared and killed on the 14th of Nisan, and also the 14th was a day to prepare for the 15th, which was an annual Sabbath wherein no work was to be done. Thus, because of a law that a body could not hang or remain on a tree (stake or wood cross) during the night, but must be taken down the very same day (Deut 21:23; cf Josh 8:29; 10:26-27). "The Jews therefore ... besought Pilate ... that he might be taken away." (John 19:31)

(16) Therefore Christ was quickly buried before sunset, before the annual Sabbath of the 15th. (John 19:40-42; Luke 23:53-55; Mark 15:42; Matt 27:57-61)

(17) Right after the burial "they returned" to their houses (Luke 23:56, 1st part of verse).

15th of Nisan, a Thursday, Annual Sabbath, 1st Sabbath of the Week

gn14» This was day of the annual Sabbath, a "high day" or festival Sabbath for Jews (John 19:31; Mark 15:42; Luke 23:54).

16th of Nisan, a Friday

gn15» After this one annual Sabbath (the 15th) some women bought spices, and they prepared these spices and the ointments that Mary Magdalene had saved (John 12:7). (Mark 16:1; Luke 23:56, middle part of verse)

17th of Nisan, a Saturday, 7th day Sabbath, 2nd Sabbath of the Week

gn16» Jesus was then resurrected on the last of the evening, just before or at sunset, on the second Sabbath of the week. He laid in the tomb from late Wednesday evening to late Saturday evening, three days and three nights as he said he would in Matthew (Matt 28:2-4; 12:38-40; Matthew 27:63; and Mark 9:31)

Note: The resurrection of the dead saints and the dividing of the door [veil] to the holy of holies occurred with the resurrection of Christ at the end of the

7th day Sabbath when the earthquake happened. (Matt 27:51-54) There was only one earthquake.

Second Week with two Sabbaths

18th of Nisan, a Sunday

Mat 28:1 "Now *after* the Sabbaths [15th & 17th of Nisan], it being morning toward the first of the Sabbaths" of the next week of also two Sabbaths.

Jesus ascends to His Father sometime after or at sunrise after greeting the women. In four days Jesus fulfills Genesis 4th day of creation: Gen 1:14-19.

19th of Nisan, a Monday, 2nd day of week

20th of Nisan, a Tuesday, 3rd day of week

21st of Nisan, a Wednesday, 4th day of week, an annual Sabbath, 1st Sabbath of the next Week

22nd of Nisan, a Thursday, 5th day of week,

23rd of Nisan, a Friday, 5th day of week

24th of Nisan, a Saturday, 7th day Sabbath, 2nd Sabbath of the Week

Notes

www.ingramcontent.com/pod-product-compliance
Lightning Source LLC
Chambersburg PA
CBHW071220090426
42736CB00014B/2910

* 9 7 8 1 6 1 9 1 8 0 2 9 1 *